"Professor Ernst's new concept—the political dead zone—will change the way people think about environmental politics. This book is a must-read for anyone concerned with environmental protection."
—ROBERT F. KENNEDY JR.

Praise for Howard Ernst's earlier book, *Chesapeake Bay Blues*
"Howard Ernst paints a stunning portrait of the Chesapeake Bay with a broad brush, yet fills the canvas with documented details of challenges to water quality, living resources, and management programs. The text is written with energy and conviction without being melodramatic. A most valuable contribution to a growing library on the Bay."
—GERALD L. BALILES, former governor of Virginia

"Ernst's book is a fast and engaging read. I picked it up before a transatlantic flight and wound up staying up all night reading."
—ANGUS PHILLIPS, *Washington Post*

"[Ernst's] recent book, *Chesapeake Bay Blues*, cuts through the rhetorical muck, which, like the algae that blooms in the bay, tends to shut out the light."
—GORDON C. MORSE, *Washington Post*

"When I finished reading this chapter and the whole book, I was much less naïve about the political process and the power of money and jobs in decision-making . . . If you call yourself an environmental educator, you better grasp some of Ernst's ideas as soon as possible."
—DR. CLIFFORD E. KNAPP, *Journal of Environmental Education*

"Ernst presents complex ideas and concepts in detail while still making them accessible to beginning students or interested laypersons—no small task."
—SUSAN E. BRAZER, *Library Journal*

"Howard Ernst's book is an original and needed view of the long struggle to restore the Chesapeake Bay to health. It's readable and thoughtful. I'd recommend it to anyone interested in the Bay, or in environmental restoration in general."
—TOM HORTON, *Baltimore Sun*

"*Chesapeake Bay Blues* is an exceptionally rich and insightful analysis . . . The book offers a highly readable and well-informed account of threats to the Bay's health and what might be done to restore both the ecosystem and the enormous economic values it brings to the region."

—Dr. Michael Kraft, University of Wisconsin

"This splendidly written, carefully documented account of the ecological and economic devastation of one of the nation's great resources is a sad commentary on the human race."

—Dr. Grace Bush, *Ecology*

"This book is very well written and provides an easily understandable description of the political challenges faced by those proposing new or more stringent environmental regulations."

—Roger Burke, *Journal of Environmental Quality*

Fight for the Bay

Fight for the Bay

Why a Dark Green Environmental Awakening
Is Needed to Save the Chesapeake Bay

Howard R. Ernst

ROWMAN & LITTLEFIELD PUBLISHERS, INC.
Lanham • Boulder • New York • Toronto • Plymouth, UK

Published by Rowman & Littlefield Publishers, Inc.
A wholly owned subsidiary of The Rowman & Littlefield Publishing Group, Inc.
4501 Forbes Boulevard, Suite 200, Lanham, Maryland 20706
http://www.rowmanlittlefield.com

Estover Road, Plymouth PL6 7PY, United Kingdom

British Library Cataloguing in Publication Information Available

Library of Congress Cataloging-in-Publication Data

Ernst, Howard R., 1970–
    Fight for the Bay : why a dark green environmental awakening is needed to save the Chesapeake Bay / Howard R. Ernst.
        p. cm.
    Includes bibliographical references and index.
    ISBN 978-0-7425-6323-0 (cloth : alk. paper)—
    ISBN 978-0-7425-6324-7 (pbk. : alk. paper)—
    ISBN 978-1-4422-0168-2 (electronic)
    1. Environmental protection—Chesapeake Bay Region (Md. and Va.)—Citizen participation.   2. Water quality management—Chesapeake Bay Watershed.
3. Chesapeake Bay (Md. and Va.)—Environmental conditions.   4. Green movement—Chesapeake Bay Region (Md. and Va.)   I. Title.
TD225.C43E76 2010
363.7009163'47—dc22   2009031111

Printed in the United States of America

Chesapeake Bay
16,000 BC[1]–20?? AD

1. The Chesapeake Bay began to take shape 18,000 years ago at the end of the Pleistocene period (the last Ice Age). From this period forward, average temperatures rose by 20 degrees, leading to sea level rise and the creation of the modern Chesapeake Bay. The Chesapeake Bay has maintained its current dimensions for roughly 3,000 years and was once considered one of the most bountiful marine environments on earth. As the health of the Bay has rapidly declined for more than one hundred years, many now fear what the future holds for the Bay.

Contents

Preface

In Dealing with the State we ought to remember that its institutions are not aboriginal, though they existed before we were born; that they are not superior to the citizen; that every one of them was once the act of a single man; every law and usage was a man's expedient to meet a particular case; and that they are all imitable, all alterable; we may make as good, we may make better.

—Ralph Waldo Emerson (1876)[1]

The mind's ability to store useful information is surprisingly limited. While people can archive significant amounts of material in the dusty basement of the mind (the subconscious), the amount of information that is available for use at any given moment (names, places, and ideas) is remarkably small. Take a moment and try to recall what you ate for breakfast yesterday morning, or for that matter, this morning? Without checking your pockets, do you know with certainty the location of your keys? Where is your wallet? Can you remember your mother's middle name?

Appreciating the limits of rational recall, I began the process of writing this book by intentionally not writing. For a few weeks, I thought about the book, but did not allow myself the benefit of putting my ideas on paper. The process of not writing forced me to concentrate on the subject and eventually little else. First the title, a snap shot for the project, decided on after days of contemplation and after rejecting dozens of alternatives. Then an outline, chapters, theories, evidence, refined theories, more evidence, a revised outline—but no words on paper—only what I could keep in my mind at any given moment. The practice was more meditation than scholarship and after a while became maddening. The idea was to use the limits of my memory to distill the project to its essential parts, eliminating waste and revealing the true essence of the project.

But at some point the process of "not writing" becomes an unbearable burden and ideas need to be translated into words on paper. For this book, the writing process began on a cold day in January of 2008. The starting point was not selected for its significance, but for practical reasons—my mind was "full," and I had the day off due to a federal holiday. The holiday was Martin Luther King Day, and it was to be a day devoid of professional obligations, perfect for beginning the process of unloading the mountain of ideas that had accumulated in my mind, ideas that were now disrupting my sleep and seriously affecting my ability to concentrate on other matters.

But like so many things in life, the day began with an unexpected twist. My oldest child, Simon, just five years old and filled with youthful curiosity, was also given the day off from "work," in his case kindergarten. To my surprise, Simon was more concerned than excited about the prospect of staying home. He wanted to know more about this holiday, and let loose with a barrage of youthful questions: "Who is Martin Luther King?" Simon asked. "Is he a really a king? Why doesn't he want me to go to school today? Can I write him a letter?" And around and around we went.

How do you explain to a five-year-old, eating Cheerios and wearing footed pajamas, about civil rights? How do you explain the concept of slavery and the lingering legacy of slavery—racism and discrimination? The long-delayed writing process was to be delayed a while longer. We eventually made our way to the basement of our home, where I played for Simon a clip of Dr. King's iconic "I Have a Dream" speech. Simon watched the screen, and I watched Simon. My hair stood up on end as I listened to Dr. King's urgent pleas to end racial discrimination and saw his familiar image reflected in the eyes of my son. When it was over, Simon turned to me and asked with all sincerity, "Daddy, do people come in any other colors?"

My son's point of reference was a crayon box, not racism. While he understood all the words, he had no way to process the meaning of King's speech. For one particular boy, King's dream had become reality, and in the process, King's words had lost their meaning. With this irony in mind and not sure whether my efforts to help my son understand had done more harm than good, I made my way up to the attic of our home to begin work on this book. On my way up the stairs I asked myself, would the concept of "sustainability," an idea that seems so new and challenging today, ultimately become so well accepted that it too will lose its meaning to future generations? Will Simon, who one year later would sit on the same couch and watch the inauguration of the nation's first African American president, some day experience the same difficulty explaining environmental degradation, apathy, and inaction to his children that I had explaining racial discrimination to him? One can only hope.

For readers familiar with my previous work on the subject, rest assured this book is not a rewrite or update of *Chesapeake Bay Blues*. The earlier work was intended as a regional case study, a wake-up call to the Chesapeake Bay's environmental community. It was a warning that politics as usual for the Chesapeake Bay would most likely lead to results as usual for the Bay, which I argued was not a good thing. That work challenged the environmental community to recognize the political factors that frustrate environmental innovation. *Chesapeake Bay Blues* revealed a stark political landscape, one in which political symbolism had become an acceptable substitute for meaningful environmental policy, where inaction was the norm, and where environmental degradation was the typical outcome.

In my earlier work, I stated what I considered to be common sense: the Chesapeake Bay was dying, and the political system was ultimately responsible for its death, which in our democratic system means we were all responsible. What I learned since writing *Chesapeake Bay Blues* is that there is often nothing more controversial than stating the obvious. With just 64,000 words, one for every square mile in the watershed, *Chesapeake Bay Blues* caused quite a disturbance. Its findings were discussed by every major news organization in the region and broadcast on National Public Radio. It led to invitations to testify before Congress and to deliver more public lectures than I could possibly deliver, or at least more than my wife would permit.

Chesapeake Bay Blues received "98 percent" approval from the Bay's environmental community. That is, the environmental advocates (government organizations, interest groups, research centers, educators, and other environmental advocates) agreed with the major thrust of the book, but inevitably took exception with the small portion of the book that focused on their specific efforts. I learned that it is one thing to criticize a restoration in general, but it is something altogether different for good-intentioned people to accept the idea that as active citizens in a democratic society and as restoration "partners," they too share responsibility for the decline of the Bay.

If *Chesapeake Bay Blues* was common sense, these are the crisis papers. The purpose of this work is to take the lessons of the troubled Chesapeake and make them accessible to people struggling with their own restoration projects, and to help sustain them and guide them in their efforts. The essential fact of our time is that no matter where we live in the modern world, we live near ecological treasures that are severely degraded. Whether it is the Florida Everglades, Puget Sound, Tampa Bay, Long Island Sound, the Great Lakes, or the Gulf of Mexico, whether we live in the Catskills, the Rockies, or the Great Plains, we live in degraded environments in which thoughtful people are working to heal environmental wounds. The lessons of one of the world's oldest and largest restoration efforts, those from the Chesapeake Bay, are lessons for the nation and the world.

What is unique about the Chesapeake Bay restoration effort is that it occurred here earlier, with more energy, more optimism, and more resources than just about anywhere else on the face of the earth. Moreover, the Bay restoration effort is the standard-bearer for a particular type of environmental restoration, often referred to as cooperative partnerships, which are now being implemented across the country and emulated around the globe. Should this type of restoration effort fail here, in a region with unprecedented levels of scientific knowledge, a strong environmental ethic, robust political support, and considerable wealth, it is unlikely to succeed in areas where the political and social conditions are less favorable. As we move forward in our effort to address the world's great environmental challenges (e.g., climate change, marine resource management) and seek to identify environmental management approaches that work, a great deal can be learned from the troubled Chesapeake.

For a system as noble and resilient as the Chesapeake, death does not happen all at once. There will be no funeral for the Bay, no obituary to announce its passing. But make no mistake; more than fifty years of raw greed, political hypocrisy, and ineffective light green environmental advocacy have taken its toll on the Bay. The once-mighty Chesapeake Bay has become a grotesque ecological zombie, a sort of living dead. It may not be dead in a technical sense; things still survive in the Bay, and if humans left tomorrow it would recover, but today the Chesapeake Bay is functionally dead.

In a functionally dead ecosystem, you can still eat some fish, but you'd better check your state's fish consumption advisory list,[2] especially if you are pregnant, nursing, or a small child, and you would be wise to wear gloves when handling them.[3] You can swim in some of its waters some of the time, but not the Elizabeth River, Patapsco River, or Anacostia River,[4] and it is prudent to avoid the Bay entirely after a substantial rainfall[5] or if you have a cut or compromised immune system.[6] A functionally dead Chesapeake is one in which majestic skipjacks are more likely to be seen in nautical museums than working the Bay's water; where community crab feasts have been replaced with weenie roasts and where wealthy tourists eat imported crab under the misleading label "Maryland-style" crabs; where once-proud watermen are forced to take jobs as prison guards on the shore or, if they try to stay on the water, become reliant on government assistance for their very survival.[7] Yes, the Bay is functionally dead.

From a political perspective, a functionally dead ecosystem is one in which necessary policies have been delayed so long and the price of restoration has grown so large that true restorative policies are not taken seriously. It is not that reversing ecological decline is impossible; it is that the policies that could bring about this type of change have become economically and politically impractical. Years of neglect have exponentially increased the price of restoration. Necessary policies today not only have to improve future land use practices and management efforts, but they also have to correct the impact of decades of environmental neglect and foot dragging. The current population is not only asked to mitigate the environmental impact of their lives, but to atone for the sins of previous generations. And as the population continues to increase and its appetite for material things continues to grow, political realities take hold. Politicians still talk about returning the Bay to pre-1950s conditions, especially around election time, but their policy initiatives do not reflect a sincere commitment to restoration. They continue to delay, adding to the price and making restoration even more difficult.

To say that North America's largest estuary is functionally dead is not to give up on the restoration effort, as some will undoubtedly suggest. On the contrary, to take the rose-colored glasses off and to see the Bay and the Bay restoration effort for what they have become is the only meaningful way forward. Brutal honesty might not be enough to awaken the long-slumbering policy process, but if nothing else it will sharpen our senses and make us aware of the undeniable consequences of continued inaction.

Acknowledgments

The story of the Chesapeake's political dead zone is not "my story," but the story of the thousands of environmental activists who have had their hard work and energies stifled by a political process that is better suited to resolve conflict than it is to produce tangible environmental outcomes. For that reason, I chose to include contributions from a small group of activists who have worked on the front lines of the restoration and protection effort. By no means do they represent the totality of the good folks struggling against incredible odds for sensible policies; no book could do justice to the countless people who have sincerely toiled within the dead zone for the sake of "the Bay."

The cases highlight shining examples of those who are willing to fight for environmental protection. They worked within the light green paradigm when possible, challenged it when necessary, made use of every reasonable tool within their arsenals of influence, and even invented some new ones along the way. The entries include a husband and wife team (Tyla Matteson and Glen Besa) who have fought for over a decade to protect the Mattaponi River from an ill-conceived reservoir project; a carpenter (Mike Shay) whose "queen of sprawl" puppet and other innovative media tactics have helped raise public awareness and helped protect open spaces in rural Maryland; a state senator (Gerald Winegrad) who fought the system from within and overcame tremendous opposition to pass the state's phosphate detergent ban; a soft-spoken environmental advocate (Anne Pearson) who has tirelessly worked to bridge the gap between property rights and environmental rights; and "the preacher of the Patuxent" (Bernie Fowler), who has come to represent the soul of the Bay. It is my honor to include entries from each of these environmental champions.

At Rowman & Littlefield Publishers, I would like to thank Jonathan Sisk for recognizing the importance of the subject and for allowing the project to evolve over time. I am grateful to my old friend Larry Sabato at University of Virginia's Center for Politics for his continued support and encouragement of my research. I would also like to acknowledge my colleagues in the Political Science Department of the United States Naval Academy for supporting my unconventional teaching and research interests, as well as the librarians at Nimitz Library. I am indebted to the numerous journalists who have taught me the importance of environmental journalism, including David Fahrenthold, Peter Whoriskey, Pam Wood, Angus Phillips, Terence Smith, Hedrick Smith, Eric Smith, E. B. Furgurson III, Timothy Wheeler, Karl Blankenship, Sandra Martin, Gretchen Parker, Rona Kobell, and Tom Horton. I would also like to acknowledge my partners in the environmental science community: Walter Boynton, Tom Simpson, Tom Fisher, and Bill Dennison. While they always seem one "causal arrow" away from understanding what is really killing the Bay, my work is not possible without their insights. I am particularly thankful for my friends in the environmental community who have inspired me over the years: Fred Kelly, Scott Hymes, Erik Michelson, Brian Frosh, Fred Tutman, V. K. Holtzendorf, Steve Carr, Ann Swanson, Stephen Barry, Chuck Fox, Al Wurth, Preston Padden, Lonnie Moore, Bob Gallagher, and so many others. Thank you to the eco-warriors of my environmental politics classes (Dark Greens, Light Greens, and Cornucopians alike) who helped me refine and enlarge the ideas that appear in these pages, in particular James Phalan, Adam Aliano, Elizabeth Byers, Adrian Andrade, Christian Burnett, and Amanda Schoenthaler. Thank you to Melisa Stango for her editorial suggestions. I am forever grateful to my lifelong research partner, my wife Tracey Ernst; this book is written for our three children: Simon, Emily, and Charlie.

CHAPTER ONE

The Political Dead Zone

Coming to Terms with the Destructive Politics of Light Green Environmentalism

Conservation is paved with good intentions which proved to be futile, or even dangerous, because they are devoid of a critical understanding either of the land, or of economic land use.

—Aldo Leopold (1949)[1]

Scientists have a solid understanding of the factors that rob coastal waters of oxygen and that are ultimately killing the Chesapeake Bay and ecosystems like the Bay. It is a process that affects 65 percent of the nation's estuarine surface area[2] and that plagues coastal waters around the globe. The scientific community has identified more than 400 of these trouble spots, or "dead zones," around the world, a number that has doubled every decade since the 1960s and now affects nearly 95,000 square miles of coastal waters.[3] The dead zone in the Gulf of Mexico has grown to the size of New Jersey and the one in the Baltic Sea is now the size of Denmark.[4] There are dead zones off the coasts of the United States, India, Japan, Australia, Brazil, Mexico, and in just about every region of the world that has polluted water and intensive agricultural production.

Parents who own fish tanks understand the basics of the problem. They know that if you leave a child alone with live fish and a can of food, the child will inevitably overfeed the fish, and within a matter of days the tank will become a cloudy mess. Like unsupervised children, modern society is "overfeeding" its coastal waterways, leading to similar results. Under natural conditions, organic material feeds a healthy supply of tiny aquatic vegetation (phytoplankton) and underwater grasses, functioning as nature's fertilizer. Such nutrients are a critical ingredient of the estuarine ecosystem, fueling a process that transforms sunlight into vegetation and that forms the base of the marine food pyramid. It was the Chesapeake Bay's nutrient-rich waters that made it one of the most productive ecosystems on earth, and it is an excess of nutrients that now threatens the Chesapeake Bay, the Gulf of Mexico, and similar marine environments around the globe.

Modern human activities cause nutrients (nitrogen and phosphorus) to enter ecosystems like the Chesapeake Bay in massive quantities. They are the by-product of agricultural production, sewage waste, storm-water runoff, and combustion engines. They enter the water through the air, streams, and groundwater. The nutrients overfertilize phytoplankton, causing massive algae blooms. When the algae die, they fall to the bottom of the water column and decompose in a process that consumes dissolved oxygen. Too many nutrients lead to a complete depletion of dissolved oxygen and to water conditions that cannot support life. Tom Horton and William M. Eichbaum explain the result this way: "the bottom line is massive regions of the Bay may become as devoid of oxygen as the surface of the moon,"[5] and without oxygen the Bay is as lifeless as the moon; large portions of it become a *dead zone*.

For over twenty years the primary effort to "save the Bay" has essentially been an effort to reduce nutrients so that the Bay can support a vibrant marine population. The numerous methods for removing nutrients are well established and include applying technologies that remove nutrients from sewage, implementing agricultural best management practices, removing nutrients from household products (like detergents), and protecting forested lands that absorb nutrients before they enter the Bay.[6] While the natural science techniques for addressing nutrients are well known, the social science understanding of why these practices are not more widely implemented is less clear. In other words, what are the forces that drive the "political dead zone"? This chapter shows that the political process mirrors the natural process in many important ways. One of these ways is that too much of a good thing, like too many nutrients, can have profoundly negative political consequences.

Environmental Conflict: A Clash of Values

To begin to understand the political dead zone, it is first necessary to come to terms with the source and nature of environmental conflict. While environmental conflicts are often presented as technical debates between rival policy advocates (e.g., those who favor a certain regulation versus those who oppose it), in practice environmental conflicts typically run far deeper. At the core of almost all environmental conflicts is a debate concerning values—i.e., what is the value of nature, and is the value of nature worth the cost of protection; and if so, who should pay for the cost of protection? In her excellent work on the subject, Judith A. Layzer explains the source of environmental conflicts this way:

> Environmental policy disputes are, at heart, contests over values. To the casual observer, these conflicts may appear to revolve around arcane technical issues, but almost all of them involve a fundamental disagreement over how human beings ought to interact with the natural world. Even though environmental disputes are grounded in conflicting moral beliefs, the participants in environmental policy contests rarely make value-based arguments. Instead, they define problems in terms of science, economics, and risks associated with environmental issues.[7]

To understand the political process, it is imperative that we address the essential value-based judgments that lie at the heart of environmental conflicts. A meaningful way to begin this discussion is to ask the simple question, what is nature?

This question leads to a series of related questions that make up a line of inquiry generally discussed as environmental ethics.[8] Where does nature start and where does it end? Where do we go to "experience" nature? Is there anything natural in the man-made world, or is nature simply the sum total of the things that remain untouched by humans? Is there anything natural within humans? Is the distinction between man and nature contrived or real? If it is contrived, whose interest does the distinction serve? What is the value of nature to humans? Does nature have intrinsic value (i.e., value other than the functions it provides to people)? What is lost when we destroy nature? Do humans have a right to healthy environmental conditions? What are more important, environmental rights, if they exist, or property rights?

These general questions can be directed at any particular ecosystem, in our case the Chesapeake Bay. For example, what is the Chesapeake Bay? Is it the watershed that Captain John Smith described in 1608,[9] an ecosystem that included immense quantities of beavers, otters, bears, martins, and minks? Is it the ecosystem that in 1760 yielded a single hunting party 111 bison, 114 bobcats, 2 elk, and 42 mountain lions;[10] the near Eden described by William Bird in 1737;[11] the ecological treasure that once produced 15 million bushels of oysters in a single year? Or is it the severely degraded ecosystem that now struggles to survive?

Where does the Bay start and stop? Does it include only the 200-mile main stem, or does it include the 150 rivers and streams that drain the massive watershed? Does the Bay include all six of the states with land that drains into the Bay (Delaware, Maryland, New York, Pennsylvania, Virginia, and West Virginia) or only the two "Bay states" (Maryland and Virginia) that actually touch the Bay? And how far does it extend into our lives? Do we include the watermen of Tangier Island and Smith Island as part of "the Bay," as their communities share a common fate with the ecosystem? Does the Bay include the annual crab feasts that have fed generation after generation of residents in Bay Country and that have nourished the region's cultural soul?

Dark Green Environmental Thought

While the questions are simple enough, the answers can be quite complex and have profound implications. One group of thinkers makes the case that humans are part of nature and argues that the nature-human divide is an artificial construct and ultimately destructive to both humans and nature. For this group, the Sunday collection at the small Methodist church on Tangier Island, where watermen make their weekly offering for more crabs, good weather, and low fuel costs, is the truest measure of the health of the Bay. This group views people as intertwined in a web of connections with nature. The group has roots that date back to Ralph Waldo Emerson and the Transcendentalists of the nineteenth century,[12] as well as the mid-twentieth-century work of Aldo Leopold.[13] They form the foundation of what has become known as deep ecology, or what I will refer to as the "Dark Greens."[14] Adherents of this school of thought view the degradation of nature as part and parcel to the degradation of humankind.

Dark Greens conclude that human beings have a right to clean air, clean water, and vibrant natural resources in public spaces. They insist that these rights require the same protections as other basic human rights. While the Dark Greens do not go as far as radical animal rights groups, who argue that animals are entitled to rights once reserved for humans, the Dark Greens do call for expanding human rights into the area of the environment. Dark Greens do not want to save endangered species and preserve natural environments for the sake of animal rights;[15] they want to protect these things because they believe every human has a right to experience them and that a world without wilderness and natural beauty is a world diminished. From their rights-based perspective, environmental protection is a legal right and the necessary policies should be put into place to protect these rights, even if they are expensive and inconvenient.

Dark Greens insists that the carrying capacity of nature (set by natural conditions and identified through scientific evaluations), not the desires of stakeholders or industry leaders, should determine the necessary course of action. The grandfather of dark green thought in America, Aldo Leopold, states it this way:

> Quit thinking about decent land use [read water use, air use, natural resource use] as solely an economic problem. Examine each question in terms of what is ethically and esthetically right, as well as what is economically expedient. A thing is right when it tends to preserve the integrity, stability, and beauty of the biotic community. It is wrong when it tends otherwise.[16]

Leopold and other Dark Greens posit that no person or industry, no matter how profitable or powerful, has the right to degrade natural conditions. According to this perspective, those who degrade natural conditions also degrade the human condition, and Dark Greens are willing to confront them.

Perhaps no single person embodies the modern dark green perspective better than David Brower. Brower founded and led many of the nation's leading dark green environmental groups. In 1952, he became the first executive director of the Sierra Club and helped launch the group's political arm. There he pushed the group's political lobbying to the very limits of the law, leading the Internal Revenue Service to suspend the group's nonprofit tax status in the mid-1960s. Wanting to move the Sierra Club further than its board would allow, Brower resigned from Sierra and formed the more assertive Friends of the Earth in 1969. Later he would found the League of Conservation Voters and the Earth Island Institute.

Throughout his career he confronted those within the environmental community and outside the environmental community who saw environmental protection as something less than an urgent human right. He regularly joked during his lectures that "I'd like to declare open season on developers. Not kill them, just tranquilize them."[17] But Brower had even greater disdain for those within the environmental community who benefited from the movement but who chose less assertive methods. In one of his most famous quotes, he is credited with saying "polite conservationists leave no mark save the scars on the Earth that could have been prevented had they stood their ground."[18] For Dark Greens, like Brower, the environmental movement has less to do with "saving" things than it does with asserting human rights. For them, the environmental movement is the next frontier in the larger human rights movement.

Light Green Environmental Thought

The other main branch of modern environmental thought posits that humans have a *responsibility*, rather than a *right*, to serve as the stewards of the environment. The adherents to the responsibility-based approach—the Light Greens—view nature the way a gardener might view a garden plot, as a wonderful treasure that is worthy of protection and nurturing. Should disease, drought, or pestilence threaten the garden, it would be the gardener's responsibility to work to "save the garden." Light Greens are the "savers" (save the manatees, save the whales, save the oceans, save the Bay . . .). For them, environmental protection is more of a hobby than a vocation. Environmental writer Tom Horton describes the light green perspective this way:

> They are like a good suburban pastor, who will give you an uplifting sermon, but who will not challenge the way you live or ask you to give money to the poor.[19]

For the Light Greens, environmental degradation is not so much a violation of human rights, but an abdication of man's responsibility for his surroundings. A growing number of adherents to this view can be found within Christian communities under the banner of "creation care." While leaders of evangelical groups, like Pat Robertson, once railed against left-leaning environmentalists,[20] mainstream Christian thinkers have more recently taken a pro-environment stance.[21] Like their light green secular counterparts, the creation care advocates generally believe that people have a responsibility to identify the source of the environmental problems and to appeal to the culprits' sense of responsibility to change their harmful behaviors. Whether religious or secular, for the Light Greens, education and moral suasion are the primary tools of environmental advocacy.

The cornerstone of the responsibilities-based paradigm is the belief that voluntary environmental goals, produced in an inclusive manner, and based on established science, can supersede the type of confrontational politics often pursued by the Dark Greens. The Light Greens believe that local and state government officials and their "partners" in the business community want to do the right thing, but require scientific justification and a bit of moral arm twisting to point them in the right direction. They see their approach as an alternative to the contentious environmental politics of the Dark Greens. They desire to move beyond the environmental conflicts of the 1960s and 1970s and to achieve a new consensus. For them, resolving environmental conflict is viewed as the key to advancing environmental policy, and if conflict resolution requires compromise, as it inevitably does, they are willing to compromise.

For the most part, the Dark Greens reject the approach of the Light Greens. The Dark Greens insist that environmental advocacy must move well beyond environmental education and moral suasion, and they insist that the environmental community make use of all the political tools at their disposal—litigation, lobbying, political contributions, recruiting candidates, endorsing candidates, advertising the voting records of elected officials, and even engaging in civil disobedience if needed. Their model for action is Martin Luther King and the civil rights advocates of the 1950s and 1960s, not Dr. Seuss's harmless Lorax. They have a sense of urgency and outrage. The Dark Greens are not interested in compromise, and they deeply resent those who are willing to compromise away what they view as basic human rights.

The Dark Greens remind us that it was their approach, not the light green approach, that led to the Clean Air Act, the Clean Water Act, the Endangered Species Act, and the creation of the Environmental Protection Agency. To which the Light Greens reply that laws alone are insufficient to restore environmental conditions. The Light Greens remind us that laws require public acceptance, buy-in from the business community, and enforcement by government agencies. The Light Greens insist that their aim is not to undermine the advances of the previous generation, but to build on them by increasing public awareness and building political will. The Dark Greens, however, see the work of the Light Greens as little more than a distraction from the real work at hand, which has little to do with environmental education or building political partnerships with polluters that they are determined to hold accountable.

Cornucopian Thought

While the differences between the Dark Greens and the Light Greens are real, and often divide the environmental community into rival camps, they pale in comparison to the differences between "the Greens" (Dark and Light) and what are commonly referred to as Cornucopians. The term was coined by John Dryzek and David Schlosberg in their 1998 work *Debating the Earth*,[22] and is now widely used to describe the economic-centered approach to the environment. The Cornucopians do not base their decisions on the best interests of the environment, but on their economic best interest. Cornucopians benefit from the environment by making use of it as a cheap and convenient place to dispose of their unwanted by-products (pollution) and by harvesting its limited resources. Like the Dark Greens, the Cornucopians are a rights-based group. The predominant right they aim to protect is the right to own property and the right to make use of private property in a way that allows them to compete in the global marketplace.

Though the Cornucopians might desire to behave in an environmentally friendly manner, their ultimate responsibility is not to protect nature, but to represent the economic interests of their shareholders and investors. It is not that those with this mentality are evil or ignorant, as some Greens might suggest; what drives Cornucopian thinking are short-term economic pressures and the need to remain competitive in an ever-changing market. The no-nonsense Cornucopians remind us that the business of business is to minimize production costs so as to maximize profits, not to protect the environment. Taking steps to control their environmental impact inevitably increases the short-term production costs of Cornucopians, threatens profits, and if done unilaterally can make an environmentally friendly business uncompetitive in the larger market.

The Cornucopians put their faith in the market and in technological innovation. They insist that economic growth and environmental improvement are not at odds, and refer to those who take this position as neo-Malthusians, after the eighteenth-century British political economist who predicted that the industrial revolution would lead to a population explosion, severe environmental scarcity, and human misery.[23] The Cornucopians insist that economic growth ultimately improves the environment and the human condition. They claim that while all economies go through a dirty period, as nations develop, countries ultimately enter a period in which the environment improves.[24] They ask the Greens to be patient, to trust in the hidden hand of the economy and the promise of technology. The Cornucopians live in a world without limits and are optimistic about what the future holds. Cornucopians call for a hands-off approach to environmental policy. They see no reason for government entities to address problems that the market will eventually correct on its own. What governments promise, but rarely deliver, the Cornucopians tell us the markets will provide naturally and efficiently.

The Dark Greens reject this line of thinking. They argue that no industry has a right to degrade the environment, even if the degradation is temporary, though they doubt it is. They point out that should the entire underdeveloped world, which includes a majority of the world's population, go through a "dirty period," the consequences would be devastating for the planet. The Dark Greens see a world of limits that cannot sustain a global population that adopts the consumption habits of the West. Moreover, the Dark Greens point out that developed nations, even with their advanced technology and efficient markets, continue to struggle with issues related to air pollution and water pollution, not to mention carbon emissions and toxins. The Dark Greens remind us that it is the developed nations that consume the bulk of the world's resources and that produce the greatest amount of greenhouse gases. Moreover, the Dark Greens note that developed nations did not "solve" their industrial waste problems, but more often than not they have simply outsourced them to developing nations. While the Light Greens would agree with the Dark Greens on many of these points, they prefer not to confront the Cornucopians. The Light Green preference is always to work with their business partners, to seek common ground through voluntary partnerships.

While the environmental community is divided in its approach, between those with a rights-based approach (dark green) and those with a responsibility-based approach (light green), the Cornucopians speak with a unified voice. They (whether they are commercial fishermen, corporate food producers, oil refiners, land developers, or other like groups) desire as little government interference as possible. They believe that if the government plays any role, it should be to promote voluntary programs that provide incentives to industry, rather than punishments such as regulations. They see the Dark Greens as little more than closet socialists; making use of the environmental movement to justify restrictions on property rights and controls on the economy. The Cornucopians couch their argument in terms of property rights and economic rights, and they warn of the dire economic consequences of environmental policies. What the Cornucopians lack in numbers—theirs is a minority opinion—they more than make up for in resources. Lawyers, lobbyists, and politics are the tools of their trade.

The Dark Greens, in contrast, call for aggressive government involvement to correct failures in the market. The Dark Greens point out that only the government has access to the considerable resources that are necessary to correct many of the existing problems, and only government has the coercive powers (regulatory powers) to change harmful practices. They insist that the central question is not about *if* we are going to pay for our environmental sins, but *who* is going to pay. They mock the light green incentive-based approach as nothing less than an ill-founded "pay the polluter approach," while their regulatory approach is a "make the polluter pay approach." Even under the Cornucopian approach, the Dark Greens remind us that someone will pay, in this case the general public through increased health risks and reduced natural resources. The Dark Greens argue that only government, through its regulatory powers and international treaties, has the ability to level the playing field, to enact standard rules that assure that an environmentally friendly business is not put at a competitive disadvantage for doing the right thing. Their preference for government intervention is based less in ideology than in the realization that government intervention is the only viable option to bring about the significant changes that they demand.

In a healthy political environment, these competing actors (Dark Greens, Light Greens, and Cornucopians) complement each other, each fulfilling its niche in the overall system. The Dark Greens bring a sense of urgency to the policy realm, threatening legal action, political action, and protests if their demands are not met. The Light Greens act as the environmental diplomats, working toward consensus and brokering deals between the Dark Greens, the Cornucopians, and the elected officials who ultimately make governmental policies. The Cornucopians oppose environmental rules, as would be expected, but ultimately give in when faced with the possibility of legal action, rigid environmental laws, or the promise of economic incentives. In the end, the Cornucopians would rather negotiate with the Light Greens than face the more demanding Dark Greens. When each group plays its role, the policy process moves forward, incrementally, but at a steady pace.

The Political Dead Zone

Like the nutrients that feed a healthy Bay under normal conditions but that rob the ecosystem of life-supporting oxygen when delivered in excess, an unbalanced political system can suck the life out of the political environment. The net result is a political dead zone—a political environment that has been robbed of its political will, the equivalent to oxygen in a natural system, and consequently can no longer support meaningful environmental innovations. It is a political environment in which good ideas go to die. The political dead zone is the outcome of the process being saturated by a single political nutrient, specifically the one-dimensional paradigm of the Light Greens. While the light green perspective is an essential element of a

Table 1.1 Spectrum of Mainstream Environmental Thought

	Left ———————— Middle ———————— Right		
	Liberal	**Moderate**	**Conservative**
BELIEFS	**DARK GREEN**	**LIGHT GREEN**	**CORNUCOPIANS**
School of thought	Rights-based approach	Responsibility-based approach	Free market
Values of nature	Spiritual/intrinsic	Cultural/recreational	Monetary
Rights	Human rights	Human responsibilities	Property rights
What limits human action	Carrying capacity of nature	Wise use of nature	Available natural resources
Long-term goals	Biodiversity & sustainability	Quality of human life	Economic growth
Short-term goals	Cap growth/eliminate pollution	Smart growth/limit pollution	Resource maximization
Relationship to nature	Humans are part of nature	Humans are stewards of nature	Humans control nature
Primary responsibility	Future generations	Cost-benefit analysis	Shareholders
Who pays	Polluter pays	Public pays the polluters	Environment pays
POLITICS			
Policy preferences	Mandatory/regulatory	Voluntary/incentive based	Laissez-faire
Decision making	Based on limits of nature	Consensus of stakeholders	Market conditions
Time frame for action	Urgent	Incremental	Delay
Primary political assets	Active members	Large membership base	Monetary resources
Political weaknesses	Limited monetary resources & small membership base	Inactive members & weak political will	Small membership base
Primary political activities	Testify at hearings, endorse candidates, protest, & threaten litigation	Environmental education, small-scale restoration projects, conduct studies, issue press releases, & limited lobbying	Campaign contributions, lobbying, & litigation

healthy political ecosystem, as the dominant mind-set crowding out alternative perspectives, it weakens the system's ability to achieve innovation and enact difficult decisions. What survives in the political dead zone are minor public policies that require little political will, policies that might slow the decline of an ecosystem but that are insufficient to reverse the general downward trend.

The Chesapeake Bay is an excellent case study for understanding the political dead zone, as the Bay restoration effort embodies the light green ideals and has been in existence for more than twenty-five years. Consistent with the light green approach, all actors in the Chesapeake Bay policy community are considered "partners"; there are no special interest groups, only "stakeholders." The Bay bureaucracy provides opportunities for "consensus-based" decision making. For those groups who are willing to forgo the confrontational approach—the dark green approach—the restoration bureaucracy and its corporate "partners" provide numerous financial incentives in the form of grants. Light green groups interested in undertaking small-scale restoration projects and environmental education programs have any number of funding sources from which to apply, but groups that choose to promote pro-Bay candidates or confront the political process head-on are marginalized by the light green political machine.

Taking a closer look at one of the Chesapeake Bay Program's long-time restoration partners, the Chesapeake Bay Foundation, helps to illustrate how the political dead zone works in practice. The Chesapeake Bay Foundation (CBF) is the largest environmental interest group dedicated to restoring the Chesapeake Bay, and one of the largest regional environmental groups in the country.[25] The foundation has been in existence for over forty years and currently raises more than $20 million annually, which translates into $385,000 per week, $77,000 per day, or $9,600 per working hour.[26] It claims over 200,000 members and a professional staff of more than 160 full-time employees.[27] The organization's "Save the Bay" bumper stickers, which have been produced since 1967, are now ubiquitous throughout the Bay states. From an organizational perspective, CBF is an amazingly successful regional environmental group.

But within the light green paradigm, organizational success does not come without a price. Despite its organizational prowess and the fact that it markets itself as a watchdog group, the CBF distances itself from electoral politics. The group has never endorsed a Bay-friendly candidate, never advertised the voting records of elected officials, has no political action committee, has never donated any money to Bay-friendly candidates, and until recently shied away from pursuing its environmental causes through aggressive legal action. The closest that CBF has come to engaging in electoral politics was to launch a mock campaign in 2008 to elect the seventeenth-century explorer Captain John Smith as president. Their fictional campaign included a sophisticated campaign website, campaign literature, youtube.com campaign ads, press releases, a Captain Smith impersonator, and campaign brochures,[28] but as for real candidates, CBF has never supported a pro-Bay candidate.

As a partner in the Bay restoration effort, the CBF, like most of the 600-plus environmental groups in the watershed,[29] has adopted a 501c3 (nonprofit) tax status that prohibits it from participating in electoral politics and severely limits its ability to engage in basic lobbying activities. While some well-respected environmental groups, like Sierra Club and the League of Conservation Voters, avoid the political limits by adopting a multilayered tax status that enables them to fully engage the political process, CBF has chosen not to pursue this option. It is not that the environmental groups are legally prohibited from participating in electoral politics; the reality is that the CBF has knowingly chosen a tax distinction that serves its organizational interests but that undermines the electoral function of its advocacy work.

It is important to note that the CBF does engage in some traditional lobbying and litigation. Even 501c3 nonprofit groups, like the CBF, are generally allowed to spend 20 percent of their expenditures on lobbying. Additional funds can also be spent on litigation. To its credit, in the last five years the CBF has significantly stepped up its legal action and federal lobbying. Jon A. Mueller, an accomplished environmental attorney, now heads the group's legal team. In 2008, Mueller's group issued an important lawsuit against the Environmental Protection Agency for not living up to the Bay Agreements. Doug Siglin, a federal lobbyist, now oversees the foundation's presence on Capitol Hill and has succeeded in winning significant federal expenditures for the Bay. But in the next election, when the area's worst environmental candidates paint themselves green and the Bay-friendly general public looks to the environmental community for guidance on which candidates are Bay heroes and which are Bay zeros, groups like the CBF will have nothing to say.

The problem, of course, is that the Bay's biggest polluters do not play by the same rules. Take for example the poultry industry. With more than half a billion chickens housed on the Delmarva Peninsula, chicken waste is a major source of pollution for the Bay. In 2003, *Chesapeake Bay Blues* reported that members of a single poultry family, the Perdue family, spent more in one recent election in support of proindustry candidates than the combined spending of all environmental groups across the three key Bay states during the same period of time.[30] According to Federal Election Commission records, since 1992 three prominent members of the Perdue family (Frank Perdue, Mitzi Perdue, and James Perdue) have given more than 450 political contributions for a total of more than $550,000.[31] Add the Perdue family contributions to those of other poultry providers, the Farm Bureau, land developers, homebuilders, and other industries that regularly engage in environmentally harmful activities, and one can begin to understand the policy impact of the environmental community's political inactivity.

In exchange for sitting out the electoral game, 501c3 groups, like the CBF, are exempt from federal income taxes; contributions to such groups are tax deductible to the donor; and the groups are eligible for various Bay restoration grants,[32] like those available from the Chesapeake Stewardship Fund.[33] The stewardship fund (itself a partnership between the Chesapeake Bay Program, various federal agencies, charitable foundations, and corporate donors) has allocated more than $16 million in small watershed grants to 277 groups since 1999.[34] Many of the grants are small, less than $50,000, and serve as the lifeblood for the small nonprofit environmental groups that receive the funding. While $16 million in funding over a seven-year period does little to close the $12.8 billion spending shortfall the Bay restoration effort faces,[35] the modest funding is sufficient to keep environmental advocacy groups busy and to help direct the nature of the advocacy-government relationship.

This is not to say that the restoration effort amounts to some sort of multi-million-dollar Ponzi scheme, or that the CBF has sold its environmental soul for grant money. That would be an easy story to tell, but the story of the failure of the Bay restoration effort is far more complex. All reliable evidence suggests that the CBF is sincere in its effort to restore the Bay, and the foundation pursues a course of action that is entirely logical from its light green perspective. The problem, of course, is that within the political dead zone even the most sincere and thoughtful environmental advocacy groups enter into a partnership with the government agencies that they purport to hold accountable, as well as the corporate entities that contribute to the grants that they receive. It is the kind of "win-win" arrangement that does little to restore the Bay, but goes a long way in resolving environmental conflict, and in the process robs the restoration effort of the type of advocacy that fuels political will and advances meaningful policy innovation. While it would be a stretch to call it "hush money," it has the same consequence.

Assumptions of the Light Green Paradigm

With the benefit of hindsight, it is now clear that the modern regional management effort for the Chesapeake (discussed in chapter 2) was built on a series of assumptions—a light green paradigm that now permeates every layer of the Bay's bureaucracy and that threatens the long-term health of the Bay. The cornerstone of this paradigm is the belief that voluntary environmental goals, produced in an inclusive manner, and based on sound science, can supersede politics, litigation, regulations, and the confrontational system on which American environmental politics was founded.[36] The basic assumptions of the Chesapeake Bay restoration's light green approach include:

1. The belief that nonbinding goals provide long-term direction to the restoration effort and can direct environmental decisions, regardless of who happens to hold office at any particular point in time.
2. The belief that the inclusive-collaborative approach to setting restoration goals provides all "stakeholders" an opportunity to participate in the process, increasing the chance of "buy-in" and, in turn, increasing the chance of success.
3. The belief that the key to environmental policy making is building partnerships between environmental advocates and industry leaders (i.e., stakeholders), as these partnerships develop trust, increase capacity for action, and fuel environmental innovation.

But after more than twenty-five years of pursuing this approach, with very few tangible environmental results to show, a meaningful critique of this approach is long overdue. The nonregulatory Bay Program, a model for light green environmental management, was not given the authority to limit pollution, to restrict development, or even to manage the Bay's living resources. The Bay restoration effort's light green approach includes two advisory councils, a series of nonbinding agreements, and the creation of a regional environmental agency that possesses no independent regulatory powers and no legal basis for action.

A quick example reveals the folly of this approach. At this time, the Bay restoration effort has no comprehensive or even coordinated land use or growth management authority. This is a troubling fact given that the Chesapeake Bay has one of the largest land-to-water ratios of any inland body of water on earth,[37] making it highly susceptible to environmental problems related to land use. What is killing the Bay is not the result of what is happening in the Bay, but the result of actions that are occurring on the land that drains into the Bay. Moreover, even in its severely degraded condition, 90 percent of the Bay's 40-million-acre watershed remains undeveloped.[38] As population growth increases and the pressure for new development also continues to grow, it is clear that the fate of the Chesapeake Bay hinges on effective land management practices.

The current land management laws in place for the Bay watershed are applied at the state and local level and generally only apply to a narrow strip of land that has immediate contact with the Bay and its tributaries. Both Virginia and Maryland have laws that restrict development within a 100-foot buffer of the Bay, but both states have weak enforcement records, regularly issue variances to the restrictions, and permit farming practices within a portion of the protected buffer. Pennsylvania, the state with the greatest amount of land in the watershed, does not have a similar set of laws. Most of the land management authority in Pennsylvania rests at the municipal level, with more than a third of the state's municipalities having no zoning laws and more than one half of the municipalities having no comprehensive growth plans.[39]

The state of Maryland, once considered a model for land protection and preservation, has more recently come under fire for weakening its seminal land preservation program. The state's preservation program, which predates the creation of the Chesapeake Bay Program, includes a significant revenue source (i.e., a tax on the sale of property) that is set aside for the preservation of open spaces, spaces that protect the state's rural legacy and help to protect the Bay's water quality. In recent years the fund has been raided by the General Assembly to cover shortfalls in the state's general fund. Even more troubling, the *Washington Post* recently reported that millions of dollars from the program have been allocated to replace grass ball fields with Astroturf fields, a far cry from what the fund was created to preserve.[40]

Critique of the Light Green Approach

While the Bay Program has been touted as "America's leading bay and river restoration program" and promotes itself as "a national and international model for estuarine research and restoration programs,"[41] it is important to keep in mind that this experiment in voluntary, cooperative management has not succeeded. While the restoration effort has produced a few successes at the state and local level (e.g., the recovery of striped bass, the removal of several dams that once blocked fish-spawning areas, and the protection of some forested buffers), the overall effort has failed to produce the desired environmental results. To date, the Bay Program has failed to meet the pollution reduction goals specified in the Bay Agreements and has failed to meet most of the secondary goals of the agreements. Members of the Chesapeake Bay Executive Council have conceded that they will not meet the major goals of the 2000 agreement, goals which are scheduled to come due in 2010.[42]

But environmental advocates in the region do not need to hear from the Chesapeake executive council or any other governmental body to understand the extent of the failure. Bay advocates are well aware that the Bay's once-great oyster industry has collapsed, that the crab population is overstressed and teeters at the point of collapse, and that the majority of the Bay's cherished striped bass are infected with a disease that poses a serious health risk to those who handle the fish. They know that millions of pounds of raw sewage flow into the Bay each year from antiquated sewage systems that are designed to overflow into the Bay. They know that much of the Bay's marine life is contaminated with mercury and PCBs. They have been warned for years against swimming in the Bay and its tributaries after significant rain events. They know that nutrient pollution, sediment plumes, toxic algae outbreaks, and low oxygen levels continue to plague the Bay. They also know that the Chesapeake Bay and every one of its major tributaries are listed as impaired bodies of water by the EPA.

A comprehensive study of the Bay Program, completed in 2005 by the investigatory arm of the US Congress (Government Accountability Office), concluded that despite receiving more than $3.7 billion in direct federal funding for Bay restoration projects over the previous decade and an additional $1.9 billion in indirect funding during this same period, the Bay restoration partners have failed to develop "a comprehensive, coordinated implementation strategy." The Government Accountability Office also found that the Bay Program's reports did not provide "credible information on the current health status of the bay."[43] In a separate study, the EPA's Office of Inspector General spent a quarter of a million dollars to find the Bay Program "is significantly short of its goals" and that "major changes" are required for its goals to be met. Ultimately the inspector general's office concluded that "current efforts will not enable partners to meet their goal of restoring the Bay by 2010."[44]

In short, the Bay Program has failed to meet its most important goals, has failed to effectively report the status of the Bay, and as a consequence, the Chesapeake Bay has failed to improve. In light of the recent criticism, the Chesapeake Bay Program has had little choice but to acknowledge its considerable shortcomings:

Although there are a number of smaller-scale success stories, the overall ecosystem health of the Chesapeake Bay remains degraded . . . Major pollution reduction, habitat restoration, fisheries management and watershed protection actions taken to date have not yet been sufficient to restore the health of the Bay.[45]

In the summer of 2008, the director of the EPA's Chesapeake Bay Program, Jeffrey Lape, called for his organization's long-standing moniker, "Nation's Premier Watershed Restoration Partnership,"[46] to be removed from its website and future publications and to be replaced with the far more modest moniker "A Watershed Partnership."[47] The change was far more than semantics; it was an acknowledgment that the Bay Program had lost its way.

In its current configuration, the Bay Program lacks the regulatory powers to achieve its goals coercively and the considerable resources that would be necessary to achieve its goals through environmental incentives. It can set goals for its partners but lacks the enforcement tools to achieve them. It remains mostly a voluntary program without the authority to sanction noncompliance. In the words of the EPA's Office of Inspector General, it does "not have the resources, tools, or authorities" to succeed.[48] After more than twenty-five years of pursuing the light green approach to regional management for the Bay, what the area now has are nonbinding agreements instead of enforceable laws, goals instead of pollution limits, a bureaucracy that lacks regulatory powers, and a severely impaired ecosystem that shows no sign of systemic improvement.

A growing body of evidence indicates that voluntary environmental programs in general simply do not work. A symposium of leading scholars and practitioners recently addressed the issue and came to rather bleak conclusions.[49] The investigators looked at a diverse array of voluntary environmental programs, both within the United States and abroad. The programs that the symposium considered were like the Chesapeake Bay Program in that they were "self regulation agreements that can be promoted by firms, governments, industry associations, and/or environmental groups to compel businesses to enhance their environmental protection performance."[50] The voluntary programs are a light green alternative to the command and control regulations that were put into place during the 1960s and 1970s and are viewed as an alternative to government rules and regulations. What these programs also have in common, according to the most comprehensive and sophisticated analysis of them, is that they do not work.

The research by Dinah A. Koehler, an employee of the EPA, which sponsors the bulk of voluntary environmental programs in the United States, found that while firms appear willing to participate in voluntary environmental programs, the programs themselves do not appear "to generate significant pollution abatement."[51] Thomas P. Lyon and John W. Maxwell, two scholars who generally support voluntary environmental programs, conceded that "despite government enthusiasm" for voluntary environmental programs, analysis suggests that "they are largely ineffective."[52] The first meta-analysis of voluntary environmental research, published by Nicole Darnall and Stephen Sides of George Mason University, found that participation in voluntary environmental programs actually had a significant *negative* effect on the environment:

> Our findings indicate that there is little evidence that overall voluntary environmental program participation is associated with improved environmental performance. Rather, nonparticipants improve the environment 7.7 percent more than voluntary environmental program participants.[53]

While the Symposium of Voluntary Environmental Programs did not look specifically at the Chesapeake Bay Program, it did involve the most comprehensive evaluation of light green programs similar to the Bay Program. What it found was that the light green approach to environmental protection is at best ineffective, and in some cases counterproductive. Jorge E. Rivera and Peter deLeon summarize the findings of the symposium this way:

> Overall, the eight manuscripts presented in this symposium suggest that the use of voluntary environmental programs has not lived up to the win-win expectations that made them highly popular alternative instruments of environmental policy. Voluntary environmental programs appear to have served the interests of those seeking to preempt more costly command-and-control regulations . . . Even more alarming, increasingly it appears that for the case of strictly voluntary programs—with no performance based standards, no independent certification, and no sanction—participant firms show worse environmental performance than nonparticipants.[54]

Looking back, it is clear that the Bay Program, like the more than two hundred other voluntary environmental programs that have been established by government agencies[55] in recent years, has paid a heavy price for turning its back on the "old environmental rights paradigm" of the Dark Greens. The Dark Green critique of the Bay Program challenges the restoration effort's very assumptions, and in doing so helps to explain why similar programs are unlikely to succeed. It argues that if environmental protection is a legal right, then the necessary policies should be put into place, regardless of the price and opposition by the business community. The dark green approach reminds us that environmental protection is a continuous struggle to change human behavior, and the most effective way to change harmful behavior is to use a combination of incentives *and* punishments:

1. Overreliance on the collaborative approach results in a situation in which the carrying capacity of nature is undervalued and science is viewed as just another stakeholder perspective.
2. Overreliance on the collaborative approach results in a situation in which the environmental community is treated as just another special interest group (i.e., stakeholder), rather than the defenders of the public good.
3. Pursuing consensus among "stakeholders" leads environmental managers to avoid addressing the hard issues on which consensus is unlikely (e.g., addressing the Bay's number-one source of pollution, agricultural waste).
4. Pursuing consensus among "stakeholders" inevitably replaces the "polluter pays" concept with the "public pays" concept, as polluters are almost always well represented in such systems, but the general public is typically not represented at all.
5. The inclusive approach leads to an explosion of environmental goals, goals that put lesser concerns like environmental education on the same level of essential goals like pollution reduction.

The dark green critique does not suggest that there is no place for voluntary-collaborative measures. It does suggest, however, that voluntary measures treat environmental protection as a luxury rather than a right. It suggests that overreliance on the voluntary consensus–based approach fosters a culture of complacency among environmental managers and their public and private partners. Meaningfully addressing environmental problems results in winners and losers, and inevitably spurs conflict. Industries, like the Bay's agricultural industry, require substantial regulations, and they will resist oversight. Other programs require substantial public funds, which can only be acquired from increased taxes or cuts to other programs, which will also be resisted. At the end of the day, environmental management is a continuous struggle to change harmful human behaviors, to make individuals and industries behave as if they would live forever on the land they currently occupy. Asking individuals and industries to overcome their renter's mentality causes countless conflicts. Conflict is not a failure of environmental management, but the clearest indication of a meaningful environmental program.

The Dark Green Alternative: Interstate Compacts

While environmental advocates in the Chesapeake Bay region were studying the Bay in the late 1960s, their counterparts in California and Nevada embarked on an ambitious environmental program to protect the threatened waters of Lake Tahoe. As in the Chesapeake Bay, water quality in Lake Tahoe was declining as a consequence of pressures from development and harmful land use practices. In 1969, the US Congress approved a bistate compact that had been negotiated between the governors of California and Nevada, creating a legally binding bistate environmental compact (Tahoe Regional Planning Compact) and a regulatory agency to enforce the compact (Tahoe Regional Planning Agency).[56]

As would be expected from an agency that aims to restrict land use practices, the actions of the Tahoe Regional Planning Agency were rife with controversy. In 1984 the governing board adopted a long-term plan that was resisted by the environmental community, which argued that the plan was inadequate to address Lake Tahoe's mounting problems. Since the Tahoe Regional Plan had a solid basis in law, unlike the nonbinding Chesapeake Bay Agreements, the environmental community was able to bring their case to federal court. While the two sides negotiated their dispute, a federal judge implemented a three-year moratorium on all new building in the watershed. In 1987, the sides settled on the long-term regional plan that remains in place today.

The Tahoe Regional Planning Agency set firm standards based on the unique carrying capacity of Lake Tahoe. Each parcel of property in the watershed is assigned an evaluation score, based on the sensitivity of the land. In some areas, development is entirely prohibited and in others it is restricted. The evaluation is based on criteria such as soil type, slope of the land, and the parcel's distance from the lake. The more sensitive the land, the greater the restrictions, and regardless of a property's evaluation score, mitigation measures are required to offset the negative impact of all development. Even minor alterations to one's property (e.g., building a deck or cutting a tree that is greater than six inches in diameter) requires approval from the Tahoe Regional Planning Agency.

Since the agency's creation in the late 1960s, its actions have been defined by controversy. Tahoe Regional Planning Agency is a highly regulatory body that imposes stiff fines on people and business that violate its rules. As a dark green approach to environmental protection, it is a rights-based approach, it is based in the law, and it sets its requirements based on the carrying capacity of nature, rather than the desires of stakeholders. Most importantly, it has worked. After hitting a low in 1997, the water quality in Lake Tahoe has improved over the last ten years.[57] This is particularly impressive given the tremendous development pressure created by the real estate boom that took place during this period of time.

It is important to note that the Tahoe compact is not a novel approach. The first time that a state took advantage of the "compact clause" of the US Constitution and entered into a binding agreement over a water-related issue occurred in 1922 when the Colorado River Compact was signed, an agreement that predates the first nonbinding Chesapeake Bay Agreement by sixty years. Currently there are twenty-six interstate water-related compacts in the United States, most of which focus on water allocation rights, but also several that include water quality protection programs like the Tahoe compact.[58] Moreover, the courts have consistently ruled that such agreements are not only legally acceptable, but they are the preferred method for the states to address their transboundary water disputes.[59]

Perhaps a better example for the Chesapeake Bay region of a successful interstate compact is the Delaware River Basin Compact (DRBC). The 330-mile Delaware River drains more than 13,000 square miles and receives the waste of nearly eight million people. As with the Chesapeake Bay, management of the Delaware River defies traditional political lines. In 1961, President Kennedy, along with the governors of Delaware, New Jersey, Pennsylvania, and New York, signed concurrent legislation that authorized the DRBC. The compact's governing commission consolidated the forty-three state agencies, fourteen interstate agencies, and nineteen federal agencies that had previously exercised jurisdiction throughout the river basin.[60] Unlike the nonbinding Bay Program, which merely attempts to coordinate the disparate federal, state, and local agencies, the authority of the Delaware River Basin Commission actually supersedes the authority of the other agencies.

In 1967, five years prior to the federal government's Clean Water Act and twenty-five years prior to the creation of the Bay Program, DRBC adopted strict water quality standards for dissolved oxygen and bacteria standards for recreational use, which included setting waste load allocations to some ninety municipal and industrial dischargers. In their 2008 State of the Basin Report, DRBC reports that their centralized regulatory program has delivered concrete results:[61]

- A large decrease in phosphorus was achieved by 1985
- A decrease in nitrogen was achieved by 1990
- Dissolved oxygen concentrations have increased and meet DRBC criteria
- PCB levels in fish tissue are decreasing

The overarching point is this: when federal and state officials commit to a management approach, there is no limit to the models from which they may choose. The Bay Agreements are nonbinding and the Bay Program is nonregulatory by design. There was nothing in the US Constitution or federal law that prohibited the Bay states from entering into a binding compact to address their interstate environmental concerns. Moreover, there is nothing prohibiting policy makers from moving in this direction in the future.

Conclusion

The Dark Greens insist that the future of ecosystems like the Chesapeake Bay depend more on the actions of lobbyists, lawyers, and political action committees than the results of nonbinding agreements, blue ribbon commissions, and wishful thinking. They are convinced that the road ahead will be defined by conflict, which should be acknowledged as a normal part of the political process rather than something to be resolved. They see the Bay Program as a conflict resolution machine,[62] an institution that is far better at tempering conflict than addressing the underlying causes of environmental decline. For the Dark Greens, the primary lesson of the Bay restoration effort is that environmental advocates need to firmly establish environmental rights—the right to clean air, clean water, and vibrant natural resources—or risk creating a political dead zone of their own.

The Dark Greens remind us that the light green approach failed in the Chesapeake Bay region because the very assumptions on which it was built were flawed. Despite substantial support by the general public, a solid understanding of the problems, goodwill among the region's stakeholders, support by elected officials, considerable public resources, and more than twenty-five years of implementation, the light green approach has not reversed the Bay's decline. The Dark Greens ask, if not in Bay Country, where might the approach have succeeded? Certainly not in regions where the ethic is weaker, where the science is less established, where the political will is less solid, or where the public resources are less abundant.

Despite the mounting evidence that the light green approach has not provided significant environmental results for the Chesapeake Bay and has provided few positive outcomes when applied elsewhere, it remains the preferred method of the EPA and the elected officials to whom the EPA reports. The underfunded, nonregulatory approaches are being emulated in large-scale restoration efforts like the Great Lakes,[63] Gulf of Mexico,[64] and in the twenty-eight EPA programs that make up its National Estuary Program.[65]

Moreover, the nonregulatory approach provided the basis for the Bush Administration's "Strategic Plan: U.S. Climate Change Technology Program," which intended to confront global climate change with voluntary measures.[66] The lessons of the Chesapeake Bay extend well beyond the boundaries of this single watershed and warrant a close look.

~

CHAPTER TWO

Mismanaging the Commons

Economic Realities, Bureaucratic Scoundrels, and Political Deception

Senators and presidents have climbed so high with pain enough, not because they think the place specially agreeable, but as an apology for real worth, and to vindicate their manhood in our eyes. This conspicuous chair is their compensation to themselves for being of poor, cold, hard nature . . . surely nobody would be a charlatan who could afford to be sincere.

—Ralph Waldo Emerson (1876)[1]

The dark green perspective reminds us of the interdependency of species—showing us how different life forms interact with each other and their environment in a complex web of connections. From this perspective, the fate of the predator is determined as much by its own "success" as it is by the availability and health of the prey; prey are dependent on the availability of plant life; plants, in turn, are dependent on environmental conditions that enable them to successfully capture the life-supporting energy of the sun. This perspective stresses the connections between species, including humans, to the environmental conditions that ultimately support all life on earth.

The interconnectivity that is stressed in the dark green perspective is made clear by exploring the role of the lowly menhaden. Menhaden are a small and notoriously oily fish that lack both culinary and recreational value. As toothless filter feeders, menhaden cannot be caught using traditional line-and-reel fishing techniques, though few recreational fishermen would be interested in pursuing the unappetizing fish. Making them even less appealing, a large parasite often lives in their mouths, leading some fishermen to refer to them as "bugmouth." Native Americans, who did not eat the fish but instead used them as fertilizer in their cornfields, had an even less appealing name for them—*munnawhatteaug* (manure fish).[2]

But from an ecological perspective, the fish is priceless. With the nearly complete collapse of the Bay's oyster population, the menhaden remain the Bay's last great filter feeder, consuming massive quantities of algae and phytoplankton and in the process helping to mitigate the harmful effects of the Bay's excess nutrients. The menhaden also serve as an important food source for many of the Bay's more desirable fauna, including the striped bass and bald eagle. In short, the menhaden not only help clean the Bay, they also sustain many of the Bay's other living resources, and the future of the Bay depends on a large and healthy menhaden population.[3]

Despite its ecological importance to the Bay, the menhaden is now the region's most heavily harvested marine resource. In 2006, 376 million pounds of menhaden were taken from Virginia and Maryland waters,[4] which is larger than the annual harvest of all Bay species combined, including the blue crab, which now yields an annual harvest of around 42 million pounds.[5] The annual menhaden catch equates to about fifty pounds of fish for every man, woman, and child in the state of Virginia.

The bulk of the fish are taken from a relatively small fishing fleet based out of Reedville, Virginia. Making use of fishing techniques that have long been banned in Maryland, fishermen in Virginia employ spotter planes to locate the fish and massive fish nets to catch the menhaden. The catch is then taken to a processing plant that is owned and operated by Omega Protein. The oils contain omega-3 fatty acids, which are used as a dietary supplement, and the remaining fish meal is sold as feed for livestock and as fertilizer for crops, much of which eventually finds its way back to the Bay in the form of nutrients.

Permitting the harvest of hundreds of millions of pounds of menhaden was liable to wreak havoc on the Bay's ecological balance, but researchers are just beginning to come to terms with the full impact of the Virginia menhaden harvest. While the adverse impact on Bay water quality is still a matter of scientific debate, the fishery's impact on other marine species is becoming clear. Researchers estimate that under natural conditions, menhaden make up 70 to 80 percent of the diet of striped bass.[6] In the absence of a plentiful supply of menhaden, the Bay's striped bass are taking on the physical appearance of fish that have been starved.[7] Some in the Bay community also speculate that the fall of the Bay's crab population is the result of striped bass, which once fed on menhaden, now turning to juvenile crabs as a major food source.

It is also believed that as many as 70 percent of the Bay's now-stressed striped bass population are infected with a disease known as mycobacteriosis. The condition is commonly referred to as "fish handler's" disease[8] and is a wasting disease that makes the fish lose weight, degrades their internal organs, and causes lesions on their skin. While its effect on wild populations is still debated, it has proven to be fatal in aquarium-raised fish. Officials are confident that people cannot contract the disease from eating properly cooked striped bass, though they warn that people can become infected through direct contact with fish, and eating raw striped bass is discouraged.[9] Though the scientific community has yet to reach a consensus regarding the exact cause of mycobacteriosis in the Bay's striped bass population, a popular theory reported in the *Bay Journal* posits "that the huge number of striped bass in the Bay are stressed, and therefore susceptible to disease, because they don't have enough to eat. Their most important prey item, menhaden, is in short supply."[10]

From the dark green perspective, it is not surprising that species suffer from having their primary food supply decimated and their environment polluted. Essentially, menhaden are the natural regulators of the Bay, filtering its water and feeding its fauna. In the following section we will see that the dark green (or ecological) perspective can also be applied to the political world. In other words, those who desire effective political solutions to materialize from a decimated regulatory bureaucracy and enfeebled political system desire something that exists neither in the animal world nor in the human world. Just like the menhaden in the Bay, which regulate the Bay's health through their very existence, the political system cannot function effectively without a healthy regulatory body.

Environmental Economics 101

Before addressing the political ecology of resource management, it is necessary to explore a few ideas that are central to environmental economics and resource management. This line of inquiry starts with the basic question, why bother with resource management in the first place? In other words, why do we need environmental regulations? If the market efficiently controls natural resources without external government manipulation, through pricing and other market forces, then environmental resource management, which amounts to little more than external market controls, is unnecessary. But if the unfettered market is unable to efficiently price environmental goods, then resource management (i.e., external market controls) is essential for the protection of natural resources and the long-term health of the human race, which ultimately relies on natural resources for its survival.

Because we are active participants in a consumer economy, the basics of economics are ingrained in our collective psyche. We understand that a modern market is the coming together of consumers and producers to exchange goods and services for money.[11] Consumers desire to obtain goods and services at the lowest possible cost. Producers, in contrast, desire to maximize their profits by obtaining the highest possible price for their goods and services. In a competitive market, competition among producers to attract consumers leads to market efficiencies. Most Americans accept without question what Adam Smith once referred to as the "invisible hand"[12] of the market—the notion that participants in a free market, pursuing their individual self-interest, collectively achieve the interests of society better than could be achieved through government control.[13]

But economists also understand that markets do not always work efficiently, and in some cases they fail.[14] A market fails to function efficiently when a price does not reflect the entire cost or benefit of a product. For example, a waterfront homeowner along the Chesapeake Bay may desire to clear-cut trees between their home and the Bay, as thousands of homeowners have done in the region, in order to improve their view and enhance the value of their property. Clearing the land would likely cost the homeowner a fraction of the value of the property, but could substantially increase resale value of the home, making the decision a rational economic choice for the homeowner. However, what is not included in the decision to clear the land is the environmental impact of such a decision (i.e., the reduced capacity of the land to filter runoff to the Bay, the increased sediment pollution, and the loss of habitat for native species). While the homeowner receives the economic value of an enhanced view, the public receives reduced water quality, degraded habitat, and diminished natural resources, a price that is not included in the market.

This type of market failure is generally referred to as an externality.[15] Externalities are the unwanted by-products created in the production of a desired good or service. In the above example, the externality is the unintended, but unavoidable, negative impact of clearing the land. Other examples of externalities include pollutants from coal-burning power plants, polluted runoff from farmland, greenhouse gases from the burning of fossil fuels, or any number of undesirable outcomes that we generally refer to as pollution. In an unregulated market, producers typically seek to pass along the cost of externalities to the general public in the form of pollution, rather than pay the price of controlling their unwanted waste. The market's inability to control its unwanted by-products is a central reason for active environmental management.

Another important market failure involves a phenomenon commonly referred to as the "tragedy of the commons."[16] In his classic work on the topic, Garrett Hardin asked readers to imagine a pasture (a commons) in which all herdsmen are free to graze their cattle. Aiming to maximize his profits, each herdsman desires to keep as many cattle on the commons as possible. Since each herdsman retains the benefit from adding cows, but shares the negative consequence of degrading the pasture by overgrazing, the individual incentive is to keep adding cows. In the absence of an oversight body that limits access to the commons (the pasture), self-interested herdsmen will continue to degrade the pasture, even though it is not in their individual long-term interest or the collective interest of the group.

The tragedy of the commons is most evident when studying marine resource management. Marine resources, like fish and shellfish, are classic examples of a commons problem. The unregulated market provides little incentive to protect marine resources from overharvesting. In fact, in an unfettered market, as marine resources become scarcer, due to fishing pressures, the law of supply and demand assures that prices will increase. As the price of a resource increases, the incentive for fishermen to harvest a threatened species to the last fish also increases, with the last fish being the most valuable. If the tragic history of marine resources in the United States has taught us anything (e.g., the decline of the fisheries in Newfoundland, Alaska, the Chesapeake, and throughout the nation's once-productive waters), it is that all commercially valuable marine resources are threatened without aggressive marine resource management.

A third important failure to consider, beyond the problems associated with externalities and the tragedy of the commons, is the problem of incomplete information among consumers. The market can only function efficiently if consumers are aware of the true price of a product, which would include the price to the environment from products produced in an environmentally harmful manner. For example, some consumers might be willing to pay more for chicken that is produced in a manner that minimizes its impact on the Bay. But lacking information about the production of chicken, consumers rely on clever marketing campaigns and price considerations when making their purchasing decisions. With a well-regulated labeling program in place, consumers would be able to meaningfully identify which products support their values, as well as their taste. But without such a program in place, consumers lack sufficient information to make informed decisions, and producers can easily hide the environmental impact of their products.

The basic problems of externalities, tragedy of the commons, and limited information illustrate the necessity for active environmental management. Environmental economics teaches us that those who desire unfettered markets and healthy environmental conditions desire something that is unachievable in the modern world. Just as the Bay needs menhaden to regulate its natural systems, the economy requires a regulatory framework to operate efficiently. This is not to say that environmental protection and economic growth are always at odds. The Cornucopians rightfully remind us that wealthy nations tend to have healthier environmental conditions than developing nations. What the Cornucopians lose sight of, however, is that developed markets do not automatically improve a nation's environmental conditions; conditions improve only after developed nations adopt necessary environmental rules. Economic development produces resources that enable nations to enact meaningful environmental rules, but alone, economic development is inadequate to produce the desired environmental outcome.[17]

The Long Struggle for Sensible Environmental Management

Given the importance of environmental management for the protection of large-scale ecosystems like the Chesapeake Bay, it should not be surprising that the region has struggled with regional environmental management for some time. Disputes over the management of the Chesapeake Bay and its tributaries predate American independence. In fact, one of the longest-running political feuds in American history, three hundred years old and counting, involves a dispute between Virginia and Maryland over which state rightfully controls one of the largest tributaries of the Chesapeake Bay—the Potomac River.[18]

In the early spring of 1785, commissioners from the states of Virginia and Maryland met with George Washington at his Mount Vernon home to discuss their considerable differences. The stated purpose of the meeting was to adopt "liberal and equitable regulations concerning said river as may be mutually advantageous to the two states."[19] The meeting, known as the Mount Vernon Conference, failed to resolve the differences between the two states, but it did lead to a second meeting in Annapolis (the Annapolis Convention of 1786), which in turn led to the Philadelphia Convention (1787), which eventually produced the US Constitution and gave birth to the federal government.

While it can be argued that a dispute over a tributary of the Chesapeake Bay helped give birth to the federal government, the birth of the federal government did little to resolve conflicts over the Chesapeake Bay and its resources. Regional competition for Chesapeake Bay's resources turned violent by the mid-eighteenth century. It was during this period that the Bay's infamous oyster wars[20] stained the banks of the Bay and its tributaries with the blood of watermen who were fighting to control access to this valuable but declining resource.

Competition between Virginia and Maryland watermen over Chesapeake oysters, once known as "Chesapeake gold," led to several armed skirmishes that eventually resulted in the state of Maryland creating its unique Oyster Navy in 1868. The state's oyster navy included nearly a dozen ships—including six sloops, four schooners, two steamers, and an iron-hulled vessel.[21] Even with this impressive fleet, the violence continued into the twentieth century and only abated in the mid-1920s after the once-great oyster population had been severely depleted.

With fewer and fewer oysters to fight over, would-be resource managers focused their energies on the Bay's remaining bounty. In September of 1924, the governors of Maryland and Virginia planned a historic meeting to discuss Bay-wide management of the increasingly important blue crab. The gathering was scheduled to take place aboard Virginia's state police steamer, anchored in the disputed waters of the Potomac,[22] but was postponed after Maryland's governor fell en route to the meeting and broke his arm. When the meeting took place two months later in Annapolis, Maryland's conservation commissioner warned the governors that "the great industry may yet be saved for the watermen in both states," if only the states would act aggressively and in unison.

Unfortunately for the blue crab, resource managers in Maryland and Virginia failed to heed the call for coordinated management, and to this day the two states do not meaningfully coordinate their management strategies[23] for their common resources. Today Virginia continues to harvest egg-bearing crabs and continues its controversial winter dredge season; both practices that have long been banned in Maryland. Even modest attempts to create nonbinding advisory committees for bistate blue crab management have met resistance. One such advisory committee was created in 1984, only to be disbanded two years later. A second advisory committee was created in 1996 and was dissolved in 2003 after proposing a modest, but controversial, 15 percent reduction in fishing pressure.[24] After more than eighty years of talking about coordinated management, the crab population has now fallen to near-record lows,[25] and the two Bay states appear no closer to coordinated management than they were in 1924. In September of 2008, the US commerce secretary declared the Bay's blue crab fishery a "disaster," making the Bay's watermen eligible for federal disaster assistance.

Other failed attempts at regional management for the Bay included a 1933 conference held in Baltimore and attended by representatives from the US Bureau of Fisheries, Virginia, Maryland, the District of Columbia, and Delaware. At this conference participants unanimously agreed to create a multistate committee to coordinate and promote preservation efforts. While the need for coordinated management was clear, the committee was never created and the participants returned to their individual states to pursue resource management in the usual manner.[26]

In the mid-1960s, the US Army Corps of Engineers launched an ambitious attempt at regional environmental management and planning. The $15 million project was designed to coordinate the research efforts of the region's leading scientific institutions, as well as the work of federal, state, and local governmental agencies. The project had three major goals: 1) assess the existing state of the Bay and its resources; 2) project the likely future condition of the Bay in 2020; and 3) recommend solutions to the Bay's existing and future problems. In 1973 the Corps fulfilled its first goal when it published a seven-volume inventory of the Bay's health.[27] In 1976, the Corps fulfilled its second major objective when it published its twelve-volume study, the *Chesapeake Bay Future Conditions Report*.[28] But when it came to turning knowledge into action, the Corps' work, like the earlier attempts at regional management, came up short.

The Corps of Engineers' project was halted prior to completing its policy recommendations, and in the late 1970s, the Corps was replaced by the newly created Environmental Protection Agency as the lead agency coordinating Chesapeake Bay policy. Rather than build on the Corps' considerable work, the EPA launched its own study of the Bay, which cost an additional $27 million and took an additional seven years to complete. Not surprisingly, since many of the EPA's research partners were the same research institutions that had partnered with the Corps in its earlier studies, the EPA's findings, released in 1983, were similar to the findings released by the Corps a decade earlier.

As the EPA released the results of its seven-year study of the Bay, nearly sixty years had passed since the governors of Maryland and Virginia had first met to discuss the Bay's rapidly declining resources (1924), fifty years had passed since the idea for a regional management authority had been hatched at the Baltimore Conference (1933), a decade had passed since the Corps of Engineers issued its stark assessment of the Bay (1973), and yet no meaningful regional planning body existed to address the rapidly deteriorating Bay.

Regional Management and the Bay Program

Convinced that the state and federal government were unwilling to enforce existing environmental laws that protect the Chesapeake Bay and its tributaries, in the mid-1970s a local government official from the Western Shore of Maryland decided to take matters into his own hands. His name is Clyde Bernard Fowler, but his friends call him Bernie. At the time, Bernie was a moderate county commissioner from a rural Maryland county and in many ways did not fit the mold of the modern environmentalist. He served in the Navy and never earned a college degree.[29] He speaks with a Southern twang and holds hands with his wife in prayer before every family meal. He is a member of the VFW, Elks Club, Kiwanis Club, Farmer's Bureau, and the chamber of commerce. His love for the Bay is not born from books or bumper stickers, but from his years growing up on Broomes Island in southern Maryland—playing, crabbing, shucking oysters, and interacting with the Bay and his beloved Patuxent River.

By the mid-1970s, Commissioner Fowler had a strong reputation among his colleagues in local government and was able to convince officials in Calvert, Charles, and St. Mary's counties to pool their resources and join in a lawsuit against the state for not effectively controlling pollution along the Patuxent River, one of the major tributaries of the Bay. In 1981, after five years of collecting evidence and developing legal arguments, Fowler and his coalition of rural counties quieted their critics by forcing the state to negotiate a legal settlement. In essence, they had proven the state's efforts to protect the river were inadequate under the law and forced the state to develop a meaningful plan to address the river's mounting environmental problems.

While it would be an overstatement to suggest that Fowler's actions caused the creation of the modern Bay restoration effort, his lawsuit certainly increased the volume of the chorus of voices calling for meaningful change. If a moderate politician from the back waters of Southern Maryland was successful in asserting his environmental rights, certainly other legal challenges were soon to follow. Fowler's bold legal action served as a wake-up call to those who were frustrated by the rapidly declining Bay and served as warning to those who resisted change. By the early 1980s many were determined that the time had come for regional management of the Chesapeake Bay; the nature of what that management structure would be, however, remained an open question.

One of the earliest responses to the renewed push for regional management of the Bay took shape in 1980, one year before Fowler settled his lawsuit. That year the Chesapeake Bay Commission was established.[30] The commission was created as a nonregulatory entity to advise the state legislatures of Maryland and Virginia and to serve as a liaison to the US Congress. Representatives from Pennsylvania were added to the commission in 1985. The commission now meets four times per year, rotating between the three states and Washington, and issues an annual report as well as various special reports. In its current configuration, the twenty-one-member commission includes five state legislators from each of the three member states, each state's director of natural resources, and one citizen representative from each state.

In 1983, with the EPA's Bay Study now completed, the Bay Commission up and running, and the sound of Bernie Fowler's wake-up call still ringing in the ears of the region's elected officials, the region's governors took notice. Maryland governor Harry R. Hughes recalls saying about the EPA study, "Let's not put it on the shelf; let's do something about it."[31] Toward that end, Hughes and his staff started holding meetings on Wye Island on the Eastern Shore of the Bay to plan a course of action. These meetings eventually led to a far larger conference held on the campus of George Mason University in Virginia. The George Mason meeting, formally known as *Choices for the Chesapeake: An Action Agenda*, was attended by more than 700 participants, including the governors of the Bay states. It was a period of tremendous excitement and unlimited possibilities. One participant in the conference, former state senator Gerald Winegrad, recalls, "I don't think there was a person there that didn't think . . . that we were going to turn it around."[32]

The conference concluded with governor Harry Hughes (Maryland), governor Charles S. Robb (Virginia), governor Richard Thornburgh (Pennsylvania), mayor Marion S. Barry (DC) and EPA administrator William Ruckleshaus signing a one-page statement of support for the Bay, which became known as the First Bay Agreement. While the agreement was short on details—the entire document had fewer than 260 words—it did call for the creation of a Chesapeake Bay Executive Council. Though its composition has changed over time, membership on the executive council now consists of the governors of Maryland, Pennsylvania, and Virginia, the administrator of the EPA, the mayor of the District of Columbia, and the chair of the Chesapeake Bay Commission.[33] While the executive council possesses no independent authority, it does hold regular meetings to discuss Bay policy, and periodically it adopts additional nonbinding Bay Agreements.

The Bay Agreements,[34] the third major component of the modern Bay partnership, are nonbinding goals that are intended to provide direction to the states, but that carry no legal weight.[35] In fact, Article 1, Section 10 of the US Constitution prohibits states "without the consent of Congress . . . [from entering] into any agreement or compact." Since the Bay Agreements have no legal authority, they do not require congressional approval and are not formally approved by Congress or even the state legislatures of the signatory states. As nonbinding documents, the Bay Agreements state general goals, but provide no consequence for failing to meet the stated goals and no basis for legal action should the states fail to meeting their nonbinding commitments.[36]

The fourth major component of the Bay's bureaucracy is the Chesapeake Bay Program, which was instituted in 1983 as a result of the first Bay Agreement, which called for "[a] liaison office for Chesapeake Bay activities" to be established at the EPA's laboratory in Annapolis.[37] The Chesapeake Bay Program, while managed by an official from the EPA and structured like a regulatory body, has been granted no independent regulatory powers. The program—which receives more than $20 million per year in funding from the federal government, has a professional staff of more than 100 employees,[38] and more than a dozen committees and subcommittees[39]—lacks the authority to independently limit pollution, restrict harmful development, or manage the Bay's living resources. Stated differently, the Bay Program is a regulatory agency with no regulatory powers; created to enforce Bay Agreements that are not legally enforceable. It is the sticky sweet stuff of light green environmentalism, but hardly a recipe for success.

Beyond the Bay Commission, Bay Executive Council, and Bay Program, a host of additional governmental entities participate in the Bay restoration partnership. The National Oceanic and Atmospheric Administration (NOAA) receives around $4 million per year to fund its Bay-related fisheries and oyster programs. The National Park Service receives funds to support its Chesapeake Bay Gateways Network, and the Army Corps of Engineers usually receives around $2 million per year for its oyster restoration work.[40]

Beyond the government entities are nongovernmental bodies, like the Chesapeake Bay Trust,[41] the Alliance for the Chesapeake Bay,[42] and the Chesapeake Bay Foundation,[43] all of which receive substantial funds from government sources.

All told, the Bay restoration bureaucracy has swollen into a multilayered, multiagency, public-private framework that enjoys considerable funding but few of the tools that would be necessary for it to successfully accomplish its restoration goals. It has no permitting authority, its recommendations are merely advisory opinions, and it possesses no legal basis to enforce its agreements. Few in the environmental community understand the distinctions between the different Chesapeake Bay organizations, which confuses the public and reduces accountability. [44] In general, environmental advocates are left bewildered by the alphabet soup of Bay organizations, hopeful that someone or some organization is actually in charge, but at a loss to identify the responsible party.

A Model of Success or a Model of Deception?

If the Chesapeake Bay was simply dying as the result of a weak bureaucracy, this chapter could end here and the solutions would be obvious. But there appear to be deeper, more troubling, and far more important questions that need to be addressed. For example, why did the political system create a bureaucracy and not empower it to succeed? Why have the elected officials to whom the bureaucracy ultimately reports continued to fund the program for decades despite the fact it has failed to meet its most basic goals? Why is the failed Bay Program being used as a model for restoration efforts around the country? In short, if the Bay Program is ill-suited to serve the public's interest, as it now appears, what individual interests might explain its continued support?

One way to address the symbiotic relationship between the bureaucracy and elected officials is to take a close look at one example of what the bureaucracy actually does and how it might benefit the interests of unscrupulous politicians. For more than a decade and a half, Chesapeake Bay resource managers have been discussing and debating numbers when it comes to the Bay restoration effort. The most important of these numbers was the 40 percent goal of reducing harmful nitrogen and phosphorus pollution from the Bay, a goal the EPA's Chesapeake Bay Program once claimed it would meet for phosphorus by the year 2000 and would come close to meeting for nitrogen by the same year.[45] In 2000, the Bay Program, as well as many of the region's leading elected officials, trumpeted the success as proof positive that their efforts to restore the Bay were on track.

After the 2000 goal came and went and the Chesapeake Bay failed to show meaningful signs of improvement, more and more people came to question how the Chesapeake Bay Program claimed that it was substantially reducing pollution, while the Chesapeake Bay itself showed little evidence of improvement. The primary reason for the disconnect is explained by a decision made shortly after the 1987 Bay Agreement was signed. While the Bay Agreement called for a 40 percent reduction in all nutrient pollution, a figure that was based on the best science of the time, that number was later redefined by the Bay Program to mean 40 percent of "controllable nutrients."[46] This new definition eliminated from consideration nitrogen and phosphorus derived from air pollution and from the states of New York, Delaware, and West Virginia, as those states had not signed the agreement. While the new definition was politically expedient, it had no basis in science. In practice, the new definition lowered the pollution reduction goal to 21 percent of total nitrogen and 28 percent of total phosphorus. By simply redefining a term, the Bay Program assured that even if it "succeeded" its efforts would not meet the needs of the Bay.[47]

The Bay failed to respond to the efforts of the Bay Program and their partners for another important reason. This reason relates to the way the Chesapeake Bay Program misused computer modeling when assessing the Chesapeake Bay's water quality. Despite its complexity, the Bay Program's computer model is nothing more than a massive accounting system in which researchers divide the watershed—the land that drains into the Bay—into specific land use types (e.g., forested, urban, pasture, cropland, cropland under best management practices).[48] Researchers combine land-use data from across the watershed with estimates of the likely amount of pollutants that typically come from each land use type. As Linda Pilkey-Jarvis and Orrin Jarvis argue in their important work on the topic, "Useless Arithmetic," one of the biggest problems associated with computer-based models is that they are only as accurate as the estimates that are fed into them.[49] The Bay Program's models are based on thousands of assumptions regarding how the land is actually being used and the amount of pollution that is likely derived from particular land types.

If the assumptions that are fed into the model are incorrect, the model, regardless of its sophistication, will yield faulty results. The more assumptions that are fed into the model, the more likely the model will produce inaccurate results. When layer upon layer of assumptions are entered into a model, as is necessary when modeling a watershed as large and complex as the 64,000-square-mile watershed that drains into the Chesapeake Bay, it virtually guarantees that the results will provide only a rough estimate of what is actually taking place in the water. While honest shortcomings in computer modeling can explain why computer models generally fail to reflect real-world conditions, they cannot explain why a government agency regularly overestimated its pollution reduction success.

Had the errors overestimated success in some cases and underestimated it in others, one could attribute the "mistakes" to simple errors in the model. But the fact that the models regularly overestimated the success of the Bay Program suggests something far more troubling. It was not as innocent as a "friendly bathroom scale" giving "a slightly optimistic result," as the executive director of the Bay Program once claimed.[50] In reality, behind each overestimate are human judgments that are better explained as the outcome of political pressures than the outcome of sound science. Take one of the most recent "mistakes" as an example—the overestimation of gains derived from agricultural land under best management practices (BMPs). While it was politically expedient to assume the BMPs were completely implemented and perfectly maintained, as the Chesapeake Bay Program's models assumed, it was not scientifically justifiable. The Bay Program chose an unrealistic best case scenario that painted their restoration efforts in the best possible light, and in doing so they provided elected officials with the positive results that they desired and that the public demanded.[51]

It is also wrong to give the Chesapeake Bay Program credit[52] for identifying its problems and working busily to correct its errors, as the Bay Program's former executive director planned.[53] As far back as 1991, in Tom Horton's first edition of *Turning the Tide*, Horton noted that the Bay Program's "accounting procedures are almost certainly overstating progress in keeping agricultural nutrients out of the water."[54] In my more recent book (2003), *Chesapeake Bay Blues*, the balance of evidence revealed that the Bay Program's "models overestimate nutrient reduction efforts."[55] On July 18, 2004, a front-page article in the *Washington Post* ran under the title "Bay Program Progress Overstated: Government Program's Computer Model Proved Too Optimistic."[56] A subsequent congressional investigation by the Government Accountability Office (GAO) reported in October of 2005 that misuse of computer modeling failed to "provide effective and credible information on the current health of the Bay."[57] As recently as December of 2007, a team of researchers at the University of Maryland found that the Bay Program once again inflated the impact of several of its key pollution reduction efforts, leading to this *Washington Post* headline: "Cleanup Estimate for Bay Lacking: EPA Program's Computer Formulas Called Optimistic."[58]

In yet another front-page *Washington Post* article, the point is made crystal clear: "Government administrators in charge of an almost $6 billion cleanup of the Chesapeake tried to conceal for years that their effort was failing—even issuing reports overstating their progress—to preserve the flow of federal and state money to the project, former officials say."[59] In his report on the subject, *Washington Post* reporter David Fahrenthold quotes William Matuszeski, Bay Program director from 1991 to 2002, as saying, "To protect appropriations we were getting, you had to show progress. So I think we had to overstate our progress."[60] Rebecca Hanmer, who succeeded Matuszeski as head of the Bay Program, stated it this way: "For us to declare defeat would mean that we would have no chance . . . of convincing the legislators to give us financing."[61]

With the benefit of hindsight, it is now clear that the Bay models served as a refuge for "bureaucratic scoundrels," a term used by Linda Pilkey-Jarvis and Orrin Jarvis in their discussion on the abuse of computer modeling in general.[62] The models were used to justify the continuation of an environmental program that had produced few accomplishments. But given the amount of evidence showing the models were flawed, even the least curious of politicians could have seen through the facade, were the elected officials interested in looking. The persistence of abuse of computer modeling at the Bay Program suggests that the agency produced results that were consistent with the desires of the elected officials to whom they reported.[63]

W. Tayloe Murphy Jr., a former Virginia state lawmaker and former chairman of the Chesapeake Bay Commission, explains, "To keep what funding you've got, you don't want to say that you just failed. So I think, from time to time, there was a little rosier picture painted." Murphy went on to say, "We never came out and said that the Bay Program office is painting too rosy a picture . . . We probably gave some slack to EPA."[64] According to the former head of the Bay Program, the lawmakers gave the agency more than a little slack. Rebecca Hanmer recalls that she was told by the Chesapeake Executive Council—the elected officials who oversee the restoration—not to declare the effort a failure: "they maintained that we should say it was doable."[65] Given the evidence, it is hard to believe that the elected officials were duped by the models; it is far more likely that they welcomed the results and put the best spin on the findings, taking credit for a virtual reality "success" story.

Another way to explore the relationship between the bureaucracy and the political leaders of the Bay states is to take a close look at one layer of the Chesapeake Bay restoration bureaucracy—the Chesapeake Bay Commission. As discussed earlier, the Chesapeake Bay Commission took shape in the early 1980s for the purpose of advising the key Bay states and US Congress on issues related to the Chesapeake Bay. Its essential function is to generate Bay-specific legislation and to help coordinate efforts in the neighboring states. Membership on the Commission is composed mostly of state lawmakers from the three states, and one might assume that its members strongly support the restoration effort.

The composition of the Bay Commission, however, reveals at least two reasons why a lawmaker might desire to serve on such a commission: one is to champion legislation that can improve the environment, and the other is to protect their constituents from environmental regulations that might negatively impact their economic interests. In 2004, an in-depth analysis conducted by Sandra Olivetti Martin, a local reporter in Annapolis, Maryland, revealed a disturbing picture of the commission.[66] Martin's study simply looked at the League of Conservation Voters' rating of each member of the commission, finding that commission members regularly voted against the types of environmental programs that they were supposedly generating. It was not simply that the commission members failed to achieve a perfect environmental voting score, but their environmental voting scores were typically *lower* than members of their legislative bodies who were not on the commission.

According to Martin's report, only three of the fifteen state legislators on the commission consistently voted in favor of environmental legislation for the period she considered.[67] Of Virginia's five members on the commission, only one member voted for important environmental legislation 100 percent of the time; the other four earned individual environmental voting scores of 23 percent, 36 percent, and 41 percent—indicating that when called on to cast a vote on important environmental legislation, they voted against the pro-environment side more often then they supported it.

Three of Pennsylvania's five-person delegation on the commission scored 20 percent, including the commission's vice chairman at the time (state senator Mike Waugh). The member with the lowest environmental voting record was the commission's chairman, Maryland state senator J. Lowell Stoltzfus, who supported only 13 percent of the environmental legislation considered to be the most significant by the League of Conservation Voters. It is not difficult to see why state legislatures might have a difficult time enacting pro-Bay policies when the majority of the commission that was created to promote Bay-friendly policies regularly opposes environmental legislation.

Regardless of the intent, we now know that the Bay Program's actions helped foster a culture of inaction that allowed elected officials to claim success where there was none, and allowed officials to put off difficult decisions—agricultural regulations, sewage upgrades, and storm water upgrades. The Bay Program and it restoration partners asked the public, through their elected officials, to continue to fund an environmental program based on its past success—success that in large part was fabricated. For their part, the elected officials were rewarded by taking credit for a "successful" program that carried very little political cost. The small-scale grants for environmental groups kept flowing, and the scientific community was kept active studying the Bay. For a while at least, the scheme seemed to work. The public was confident the Bay was improving, the elected officials could tout their environmental accomplishments, and the Bay Program's funds continued to flow. But all the while, the Chesapeake Bay continued its gradual decline —an environmental disaster unfolding in slow motion.

The Sticky Sweet Stuff of Light
Green Political Promises

When Barack Obama and John McCain addressed their respective supporters on February 11, 2008, the day before the presidential primaries in Maryland and Virginia, both candidates carried on a longstanding tradition in the region—they both pledged their unwavering support to restore the Chesapeake Bay. Speaking to a group of more than seventeen thousand supporters at the Comcast Center at the University of Maryland, Senator Obama declared that "we cannot wait to clean up Chesapeake Bay." That same day, Senator McCain, speaking to a smaller crowd in Annapolis, promised, "I will do everything in my power to make sure we repair and improve one of the great national treasures, the Chesapeake Bay."

Forty-three years earlier, President Johnson promised to make the restoration of the Potomac, one of the Bay's largest tributaries, "a model of beauty." In President Reagan's 1984 State of the Union address he called the Chesapeake Bay "a special natural resource" and committed himself to its restoration. George H. Bush pledged to "revitalize" the Bay. Bill Clinton assured America that his programs would "help reclaim the natural beauty of the Chesapeake Bay." George W. Bush, prior to leaving for a fishing trip on the

Bay in October of 2007, took the opportunity to assert that his "administration is committed to protecting the environment that our sportsmen depend on."

The pledges of support are echoed by gubernatorial candidates in Maryland and Virginia, by senators, members of the US House of Representatives, and seekers of public office at every level in the Bay states. The claims of support are bipartisan and overwhelming, and ultimately inconsequential. With all candidates claiming to be green, regardless of their environmental records, and so few environmental groups willing to distinguish between true environmental champions and environmental imposters, there is very little reward for making the hard decisions that could actually improve the Bay. In this political environment, the political course of least resistance (the course pursued by an elected official who cares nothing of policy, but is only concerned with winning elections) is to pay lip service to light green pro-Bay policies that are neither expensive nor controversial, while providing polluting industries with the tangible policy outcomes that they demand.

It is not that the political dead zone kills all environmental programs; the effects are far more subtle. The dead zone produces feel-good environmental programs that are better equipped to generate public support than they are to address the pressing environmental problems of our day. Hard questions, like funding billions of dollars in storm water controls, or billions more in sewage upgrades, or regulating the Bay's single biggest polluter (agriculture) are ignored or delayed, while lesser concerns are addressed. Even the programs that are directed at "the big problems" tend to be distorted and watered down to the point that they provide little actual improvement.

For example, Maryland's agricultural pollution problem, which after more than a decade of debate was supposed to be addressed by the state's much-touted Water Quality Improvement Act of 1998, has done little in practice to actually clean up farms in the state. In 2002, the deadline for drafting nutrient management plans came and went, with the majority of farms ignoring the deadline and receiving no penalty.[68] In 2003, Maryland governor Robert L. Ehrlich Jr. abandoned "rules to hold such poultry giants as Tyson Foods and Perdue Farms Inc. accountable for pollution caused by chicken waste."[69] In 2007, Maryland's new governor, Martin O'Malley, proposed long-delayed poultry regulations but applied them to only 200 of the state's 800 largest poultry operations. And in the summer of 2008, after receiving pushback from the poultry industry, O'Malley weakened his proposed regulations by applying them to only 75 to 100 of the very largest poultry outfits.[70] As for the inspectors who are tasked with enforcing the state's environmen-

BOX 2.1
Presidential Statements Regarding the Chesapeake Bay and the Potomac River

President Lyndon B. Johnson (January 4, 1965)
State of the Union Address
We hope to make the Potomac a model of beauty here in the Capital, and preserve unspoiled stretches of some of our waterways with a Wild Rivers bill. www.presidency.ucsb.edu/ws/?pid = 26907

President Lyndon B. Johnson (February 8, 1965)
Special Message to Congress on Conservation
The Potomac . . . rich in history and memory which flows by our nation's capital should serve as a model of scenic and recreation values for the entire country. www.presidency.ucsb.edu/ws/?pid = 27285

President Lyndon B. Johnson (October 2, 1965)
Remarks at the Signing of the Water Quality Act of 1965
We are going to begin right here in Washington with the Potomac River. Two hundred years ago George Washington used to stand on his lawn down here at Mount Vernon and look on a river that was clean and sweet and pure. In our own century President Theodore Roosevelt used to go swimming in the Potomac. But today the Potomac is a river of decaying sewage and rotten algae. Today all the swimmers are gone; they have been driven from its banks. www.presidency.ucsb.edu/ws/?pid = 27289

President Lyndon B. Johnson (March 9, 1967)
Message to the Congress Transmitting First Report on Marine Resources and Engineering Development
We must . . . study the Chesapeake Bay to determine the effects of estuarine pollution on shellfish, health, recreation, and beauty, and to provide a basis for remedial measures. www.presidency.ucsb.edu/ws/?pid = 28119

President Ronald Reagan (January 25, 1984)
State of the Union Address
Though this is a time of budget constraints, I have requested for EPA one of the largest percentage budget increases of any agency. We will begin the long, necessary effort to clean up a productive recreational area and a special national resource—the Chesapeake Bay. www.presidency.ucsb.edu/ws/?pid = 40205

President Ronald Reagan (July 9, 1984)
Question-and-Answer Session with Editors on Foreign and Domestic Issues
Its [the Bay's] decline in quality—what has been done to it—just is unconscionable. And we are pledged to reverse that . . . It is a great and a very unique ecosystem.
www.presidency.ucsb.edu/ws/?pid = 40136

President Ronald Reagan (July 10, 1984)
Remarks to State and Local Officials in Tilghman Island, Maryland
This is more than an income for you, it's a way of life. And believe me, we aren't going to let anything destroy it . . . Clearly the time for action is now. The oyster crop and the crab harvest are down. Other statistics like those concerning the decline of the striped bass are also cause for concern. This is not a question of environmental concerns versus economic development. We can and will preserve the bay without hurting the economy or stopping growth. In fact, much of the economic vitality of this region depends on conserving the bay and its many resources.
www.presidency.ucsb.edu/ws/?pid = 40142

Republican Party Platform (August 20, 1984)
National Republican Party Convention
The Republican Party endorses a strong effort to control and clean up toxic wastes. We have already tripled funding to clean up hazardous waste dumps, quadrupled funding for acid rain research, and launched the rebirth of the Chesapeake Bay.
www.presidency.ucsb.edu/ws/?pid = 25845

President Ronald Reagan (October 8, 1984)
Remarks at a Dedication Ceremony for a Statue of Christopher Columbus in Baltimore, Maryland
I know there is an issue which the people of Baltimore are particularly concerned about, and it's a concern that I share. We've taken steps, with the strong support of your Senator Mac Mathias, to make certain that the new—or the next generation has a healthy and thriving Chesapeake Bay. It's a national treasure, and we're not going to lose it.
www.presidency.ucsb.edu/ws/?pid = 39203

Republican Party Platform (August 16, 1988)
National Republican Party Convention
We support a comprehensive plan of action to fight coastal erosion and to protect and restore the nation's beaches, coral reefs, bodies of water, wetlands, and estuaries such as the Louisiana coast, Chesapeake Bay, the Great Lakes, San Francisco Bay, Puget Sound, Narragansett Bay, and other environmentally sensitive areas. The restoration of these areas will continue to be a priority.
www.presidency.ucsb.edu/ws/?pid = 25846

President George H. W. Bush (April 18, 1991)
Message to the Congress Reporting on Environmental Quality
We will also seek to make progress toward the goal of no-net-loss of wetlands and to strengthen programs to revitalize the Great Lakes, the Chesapeake Bay, and other productive ecosystems.
www.presidency.ucsb.edu/ws/?pid = 19494

President George H. W. Bush (January 23, 1992)
Remarks on Environmental Policy
In EPA's budget we're providing significant increases for Superfund; implementing the Clean Air Act; for enforcing our environmental laws, and that's critical; and protecting important resources like the Great Lakes, the Gulf of Mexico, and the Chesapeake Bay: a strong program.
www.presidency.ucsb.edu/ws/?pid = 20531

President William J. Clinton (July 27, 1994)
Remarks on the Fourth Anniversary of the Americans with Disabilities Act
I'd also like to introduce three young people from Gallaudet University who are here who are part of one of our administration's most important initiatives and an illustration of why we have to keep working to open the doors of opportunity to all Americans . . . Beginning this September, they will be part of 20,000 young Americans who will be working to help to reclaim our sense of national community. They'll be working to help reclaim the natural beauty of the Chesapeake Bay. www.presidency.ucsb.edu/ws/?pid = 50556.

President William J. Clinton (April 21, 1995)
Remarks on the 25th Anniversary of Earth Day in Havre de Grace, Maryland
I'll never forget the first time I saw the Chesapeake, about 30 years ago now—a little more actually. Will your children's children see what we see now and what I saw then? Will there be water clean enough to swim in? Will there be a strong economy that is sustained by a sound environment? Believe me, if we degrade our American environment, we will depress our economy and lower our incomes and shrink our opportunities, not increase them.
www.presidency.ucsb.edu/ws/?pid = 51253

President William J. Clinton (May 16, 2000)
Remarks Announcing the Coral Reef and Marine Protected Areas Initiatives at Assateague Island, Maryland
Poisonous runoff from the Mississippi River alone has created a dead zone in the Gulf of Mexico that is as large as the State of New Jersey. Here in Maryland, runoff threatens fish and crabs in the Chesapeake Bay.
www.presidency.ucsb.edu/ws/?pid = 58554.

President George W. Bush (October 20, 2007)
Presidential Radio Address
This weekend I will join millions of Americans in one of our favorite national pastimes, fishing. I'm going to be on the Chesapeake Bay . . . My administration is committed to protecting the environment that our sportsmen depend on.
www.presidency.ucsb.edu/ws/?pid = 75936

Presidential Candidate John McCain (February 11, 2008)
Campaign Speech in Annapolis, Maryland
I will do everything in my power to make sure we repair and improve one of the great national treasures of the earth [Chesapeake Bay].

Presidential Candidate Barack Obama (February 11, 2008)
Campaign Speech to 17,000 People at the Comcast Center, University of Maryland
In such a situation, we cannot afford to wait, we cannot wait to fix our schools, we cannot wait to fix our healthcare system, we cannot wait to bring back good jobs and good wages, we cannot wait to give our young people an opportunity to live a decent life, we cannot wait to end global warming, we cannot wait to clean up Chesapeake Bay.

Source: Compiled by author from John T. Woolley and Gerhard Peters, *The American Presidency Project* [online]. Santa Barbara, CA: University of California (hosted), Gerhard Peters (database).

---

tal laws, Maryland has only 132 inspectors to cover 205,000 sites. The ratio of inspectors to sites stands at 1 to 1,500, up from 1 to 1,090 in 2003.[71]

Examples of poorly implemented or counterproductive environmental measures abound. Maryland's "flush tax," a fee on sewage and septic users for the purpose of upgrading waste treatment and funding cover crops is now blamed for actually promoting harmful development, as the money is not only being used to improve facilities, but it is also be used to expand capacity of existing plants, which in turn facilitates harmful development.[72] Funding designed to preserve open spaces in Maryland, land that protects the state's rural legacy and helps protect water quality in the Bay, is being allocated by the millions to replace grass ball fields with Astroturf fields.[73] Critical area laws, designed to protect land in the most sensitive areas of the Bay, are being ignored by developers without significant consequences.[74] The political dead zone, fueled by the consensus-obsessed politics of the light greens, overemphasizes the interests of polluters and distorts even the best of ideas.

The programs that make it through the light green system without serious alteration tend not to target specific polluting industries, tend to be nonregulatory, and tend to be costly only to the underrepresented taxpayers. For example, while environmental funds are scarce throughout the country and the Bay restoration effort faces a multibillion-dollar shortfall, the US House passed a bill sponsored by Maryland congressman John Sarbanes (D) that would provide $500 million in federal dollars for environmental education. Likewise in 2003, when the Bay Program was beginning to come to terms with the fact that it could not meaningfully address all the goals through voluntary programs and chose to concentrate its effort on its ten most important goals, the program selected providing "a meaningful Bay or stream outdoor experience for every school student in the watershed before graduation from high school" as one of its ten "keystone" goals.[75] In 2006, the same year the EPA announced it would not meet its pollution reduction goals for the Bay,[76] the Bay's environmental community applauded the region's political leaders and the president for establishing a national water trail.[77]

While providing outdoor education is a nice idea and creating a water trail equipped with interpretative buoys certainly has its place, these are hardly a pressing Bay concern on par with nutrient reductions and sensible resource management. The political dead zone is not dangerous merely because it stifles meaningful environmental innovation, though it does; its ultimate danger is that elected officials are able to take credit for symbolic environmental policies that require little political will and that do not reverse the decline of the ecosystem. In the process, actual environmental champions, elected officials who understand the problems and who are willing to make the tough decisions that are necessary to reverse the problem, receive little reward for their efforts. Education and studies continue, regulations and pollution reduction resources lag, and the Bay continues its gradual decline.

A Ray of Hope?

On December 3, 2008, an unprecedented event took place in Annapolis, Maryland. A group of twenty distinguished Chesapeake Bay scientists and policy experts crowded into a small room at the Maryland Inn to discuss the fate of the Bay restoration effort.[78] The meeting itself was not particularly significant; most of the people in the room knew each other and all the attendees had participated in similar discussions in the past. But what the participants had to say was groundbreaking. Within a short period of time, the diverse group of environmental experts agreed to a unanimous statement regarding the Bay restoration effort. Their statement declared that the voluntary/collaborative structures under the formal Bay Program had not succeeded and, as a consequence, the Bay's health was declining, not improving:

> We have concluded that after 25 years of effort, the formal Bay Program and the restoration efforts under the voluntary, collaborative approach currently in place have not worked. We recognize that many people, organizations, and government entities have worked diligently to restore the Bay, which would be worse without their actions. But in the face of significant population growth and expanding development, these efforts have been insufficient and are failing. Water quality is declining or not improving in much of the Bay and its rivers, and living resources continue to decline. We must transition from the voluntary collaborative approach in place for 25 years to a more comprehensive regulatory program that would establish mandatory, enforceable measures for meeting the nutrient, sediment, and toxic chemical reductions needed to remove all Bay waters from the Clean Water Act impaired waters list. These measures should be fully implemented and enforced so our children can safely swim, fish, and enjoy the Bay as their grandparents once did. The required reductions of nutrients, sediment, and toxic chemicals must be based on quantitative, scientific standards, have enforceable limits, precise monitoring, and substantive sanctions for noncompliance. We believe that the core of this new approach to Bay restoration should be the principles that clean water is a *right* of all citizens and that *polluters should pay*.

The December 3 meeting was followed by a press event five days later in which members of the group[79] handed their declaration of action to the director of the EPA's Bay Program office, Jeffrey Lape. The formal intervention concluded with Director Lape politely acknowledging that the health of the Bay "is not where it needs to be."[80] What Director Lape failed to realize is that the group was not finding fault with the state of the Bay; they understood the condition of the Bay. The group was condemning the state of the Bay restoration effort and the unfounded light green assumptions upon which the restoration had been built. What made the group unique is that they were not calling for more of the same (e.g., more funding, more collaboration, more consensus); what they demanded was the replacement of the nonregulatory Bay Program with a regulatory environmental management authority. Their message was picked up by major news organizations and repeated throughout the region. Pollution was not killing the Bay; the ineffective voluntary partnership that allowed pollution to go unchecked was killing the Bay.

Three months later the new Obama administration seemed to heed the call for action by appointing J. Charles (Chuck) Fox to a new position at the EPA, senior advisor on the Chesapeake Bay. Chuck Fox has twenty-five years of combined experience as an environmental advocate, a regulator at EPA, and head of Maryland's Department of Natural Resources. More importantly, he has a well-earned reputation in the environmental community as a hard-nosed champion of the Chesapeake Bay. The feeling among the environmental community was that no one was better versed in the problems of the Bay than Fox, and no one was likely to push harder within the new administration for the tools that are necessary to turn around the failing restoration program. But with the administration concerned about an economic downturn, foreign military conflicts, and global climate change, it was unclear if Fox would have the political sway to achieve the regulatory changes that could reinvigorate the Bay restoration effort.

On May 12, 2009, the governors of the key Bay states met to chart a new course for the Bay, and President Obama issued an executive order concerning Chesapeake Bay restoration. The Chesapeake Bay Foundation sent a notice to its supporters declaring the change "breaking news." They lauded the president for declaring the Bay a "national treasure" and for asking the EPA to examine how to make full use of its authorities under the Clean Water Act to restore the Chesapeake Bay. Headlines throughout the region echoed the excitement of the foundation. An article on the front page of the *Washington Post* read, "Obama Orders EPA to Take the Lead in Bay Cleanup,"[81] the *Virginian-Pilot* declared, "Obama Gives New Chesapeake Bay Cleanup a Boost,"[82] and the *Richmond Times Dispatch* stated, "Chesapeake Bay Cleanup to Be Speeded Up."[83] It appeared that at long last elected officials at the state and federal level were making the hard decisions that would be necessary to restore the Bay. Or were they?

Hidden beyond the headlines and government press releases were the raw facts. The new nitrogen and phosphorus pollution targets that states adopted were actually less stringent than the targets that scientists indicated were necessary to restore the Bay and were weaker than the previous goals that the states had set and missed.[84] The long-term goal of the new approach was to have all pollution control measures necessary for a restored Bay in place by no later than 2025, which sounds impressive until you realize that putting pollution controls in place is not the same thing as actually reducing pollution. Moreover, the Clean Water Act, which makes a similar pledge, was passed fifty-two years prior to this new deadline. The executive order provides no new funding, no new statutory authority, no new regulatory powers, and no new legal responsibilities for the federal or state governments.

What the executive order did was declare the Bay a national treasure, which Ronald Reagan also did twenty-five years earlier; it created a new committee within the federal bureaucracy; and it required the EPA to make recommendations to the new committee within four months. The "new" approach is a far cry from the hard–hitting, regulatory polluter-pays approach that the "group of twenty" demanded at their December intervention in Annapolis. It appears it is going to take time for the Bay partners to end their addiction to voluntary environmental programs. Though small indeed, the Bay restoration effort has taken the initial steps to recovery; they have acknowledged they have a problem, and they are seeking help from a higher power (the federal government).

CHAPTER THREE

Who Will Tell the People?

The Rise and Fall of Environmental Journalism

As we degenerate, the contrast between us and our house is more evident. We are as much strangers in nature as we are aliens from God. We do not understand the notes of birds. The fox and the deer run away from us; the bear and the tiger rend us.

—Ralph Waldo Emerson (1836)[1]

The word *Chesapeake* is derived from the Algonquin Indian word *Chesepiooc*, meaning "the great shellfish bay."[2] The shellfish that the Algonquin referenced were the Bay's native oysters (*crassostrea virginica*). Later inhabitants would call the oyster "Chesapeake gold," as it was the region's most valuable natural resource and one of the nation's most highly sought-after delicacies. During the nineteenth century competition over the Chesapeake oyster led to frequent skirmishes and rampant poaching.[3] By 1868, the state of Maryland created its notorious Oyster Navy to help control the increasingly violent confrontations, but it seems that nothing could curb the human greed that fueled the exploitation of the species.

The region's first oyster harvest survey, conducted in 1880, recorded an annual catch of 123 million pounds. Since oysters are only harvested in winter months (typically months ending in the letter "r," when the oyster's flesh is most tender), we can calculate that more than a million pounds of oysters were being legally harvested from the Bay per day during the winter months of the early 1880s, and untold additional pounds were being harvested illegally. In places like Baltimore and Crisfield,[4] oysters were carried to distant markets by train, sometimes hauling as many as thirteen railroad cars filled with oysters per day.[5] During its heyday in the late nineteenth century, the Bay produced more oyster meat than the cattle farms of Maryland, Delaware, and Virginia combined.[6] At this rate, even had the Bay's waters remained unpolluted and had disease[7] not spread throughout the Bay's oyster population, the fate of Chesapeake Bay gold was sealed.

As pollution increased, diseases spread, and overharvesting continued, predictably the oyster population collapsed.[8] Today the annual oyster haul is no longer measured in the millions of pounds but in the thousands, and watermen are going to greater and greater lengths to harvest the Bay's remaining oysters. The oyster is currently estimated to be at less than 2 percent of historic abundance. Gone are the trains leaving Baltimore with boxcars filled with Chesapeake oysters. Gone are the shell-lined roads that existed throughout Bay country. Gone are the oyster feasts that added to the cultural bounty of the region. What remains are a handful of watermen making use of increasingly dangerous and desperate measures, including scuba-assisted techniques that call on watermen to literally plunge into the Bay's icy wintry waters in search of the region's last oysters.[9] What also remains is an ineffective environmental bureaucracy that appears incapable of halting the remaining oyster harvest.

Pollution, disease, and mismanagement did more than kill an industry; it changed the very ecology of the Bay. It has long been known that oysters are prodigious filterers of algae. By removing large quantities of algae, they substantially improve water quality and increase the ability of a water system to support other living organisms. A more recent discovery, however, found that in addition to filtering algae, oysters actually remove large quantities of nitrogen from the water (the Bay's biggest source of pollution). Dr. Roger Newell and his coresearchers at the University of Maryland Center for Environmental Science recently found that rather than simply recycling nitrogen (i.e., consuming it and then excreting it in their waste back into the water as was previously believed), oysters actually removed as much as 20 percent of the nitrogen that the researchers introduced in their study.[10]

With the loss of the Bay's native oyster population, the system's very ability to cope with naturally occurring pollution loads has been severely weakened. Even if pollution was reduced to "normal" (preindustrial) levels, the Bay's ability to cope would be undermined. It is equivalent to turning off the filter in your aquarium. Even if pollutants are not added to the tank, without the filter it is only a matter of time before the aquarium becomes inhospitable to living organisms. The bottom line is that without a robust oyster population, even substantially reducing nutrients from the Bay may not be sufficient to correct the dead zone.

Once again, the Dark Greens would not be surprised by the fact that the destruction of one life form disrupts the overall system. In the remainder of this chapter, we apply this central proposition of the Dark Greens, the inter-connectivity of species to other species and the overall system, to the political world. In this case we take a close look at the importance of the public's great filter feeder, journalists. We explore the fall of print media (environmental journalism in particular) and assess the impact it is likely having on public discourse and the political system. In short, does the decline of environmental journalism add to the political dead zone, reducing the political pressure to address the most important environmental problems of our day? Like removing oysters from the Bay, or the filter from an aquarium, it is likely that the fall of environmental journalism has left the system less resilient and more susceptible to the ills of the political dead zone.

Why Environmental Journalism Matters

The leading environmental stories of our time are well known to the environmental community (e.g., Love Canal, Three Mile Island, *Silent Spring*, climate change, and others), but what is far less obvious is how these stories gained positions of prominence in the crowded marketplace of public concern. In hindsight, one might assume that the stories were "newsworthy" from the outset and that the barrage of media attention that eventually followed them was inevitable. But a closer look suggests that many, if not most, environmental news stories are anything but obvious and in some cases remain out of the public view for extended periods of time.

Take for example the issue of Love Canal in Niagara Falls, New York.[11] From 1942 to 1952 the Hooker Chemical and Plastics Corporation quietly dumped more than 4.4 million pounds of toxic chemicals at the site. By the 1970s the waste disposal site was closed, and due to a series of horrifically poor decisions, the site was allowed to become home to an elementary school (99th Elementary School), a working-class neighborhood, and the LaSalle Expressway. By 1976, waste began seeping into the neighborhood, literally infiltrating people's basements and pooling in their yards. Local reporters from the *Niagara Gazette* (David Pollack and Michael Brown) began investigating the story in 1976, and Brown ran a series of stories for the *Gazette* in 1977.[12] Despite attention from the local media and a growing body of evidence that the site posed a serious human health hazard to the community, virtually nothing was initially done to address the danger.

This all changed on August 2, 1978, when Donald McNeil broke the story on the front page of the New York Times under the title "Upstate Waste Site May Endanger Lives."[13] McNeil's initial story was followed up by additional coverage by the Times and a full-fledged media frenzy by national news organizations. Within days, governor Hugh Carey, who was up for reelection in November, provided rent vouchers and moving assistance for thirty-seven families with small children or pregnant women. On August 6, only four days after McNeil's story, the federal disaster assistance director inspected the site, and one day later president Jimmy Carter approved federal emergency relief funds. By the time the dust had settled, two schools would be closed and leveled and hundreds of families would be relocated away from the contaminated site. The controversy surrounding Love Canal would eventually lead to the creation of the Superfund Law (1980), which was designed to address the nation's large-scale hazardous waste problems.[14]

But Love Canal is only one example of the importance of media coverage in framing environmental stories and driving the policy process. Another example is Rachel Carson's Silent Spring, now considered one of the most influential environmental works of the twentieth century. What many people forget is that despite the success of her earlier books, Carson originally failed to attract a single publisher for her study of the harmful effects of pesticides. It was not until the New Yorker published a stylized account of her study and CBS Reports ran its exposé on Carson's work that Silent Spring became the environmental news sensation that sent her message mainstream.[15] And closer to home, it was not the findings of Turning the Tide or Chesapeake Bay Blues that ultimately exposed the Chesapeake Bay Program's misuse of computer models and inflated pollution reduction numbers, even though both of these works reported the problems.[16] Ultimately it was front-page coverage in the Washington Post (by reporters Peter Whoriskey and David Fahrenthold) that exposed the abuses at the Bay Program to the general public and set off a firestorm of investigations.[17]

The public learned about these issues because reporters and editors at the Niagara Gazette, New York Times, New Yorker, and Washington Post deemed them newsworthy. But how much longer would children have played amongst the toxic waste of Love Canal had Pollack and Brown not been interested in the issue, or if they simply did not have the time or resources necessary to uncover the difficult story? Rachel Carson's Silent Spring was built on the findings of dozens of studies that suggested the harmful effects of pesticides, though these studies were virtually ignored prior to the coverage of her book. And the misuse of computer modeling by the Bay Program occurred for more than two decades before a *Washington Post* reporter showed interest in the issue.

The fact that these stories eventually broke does not suggest that all environmental news stories receive the attention they warrant. For example, few Americans are familiar with the health risk of radon gas. Without a company to blame or a political champion to cite, this naturally occurring, invisible, and colorless gas receives little attention from the mainstream press. This is true despite the fact that the Environmental Protection Agency estimates that radon is responsible for 21,000 lung cancer deaths every year, with 2,900 of these deaths occurring among people who have never smoked.[18] Nearly the same number of nonsmokers die each year in this country from radon gas exposure as died in the terrorist attacks of September 11, 2001. Moreover, the exposure is controllable with appropriate building codes and simple remediation measures. But with little attention given to this silent killer, few states have instituted mandatory radon control standards.[19]

Environmental news matters because most people do not learn about environmental problems from scientific research reports, scholarly books, or through direct observation. Most people learn about environmental conditions through the mainstream media. Moreover, while most politicians have a general understanding of environmental problems, political actors tend to shy away from tricky environmental issues until the public has voiced its concern. What environmental journalists cover and how they frame their stories influences the public's perception about environmental problems and in turn drives the policy process. Moreover, what they choose not to cover or what they are not given the space or time to cover has an equally important impact on the public's perception and the policy process.

The State of Journalism in America

In its 2005 "State of the News Media" report, the Project for Excellence in Journalism (Columbia University) described the state of the industry this way: "journalism was in the midst of an epochal transformation, as momentous as the invention of the telegraph or television."[20] While the rise of online news is a well known part of that revolution, the Project for Excellence in Journalism also notes that other parts of the transformation include a loss of readership among daily newspapers, a loss of advertising revenue, and the collapse of the previous news-media business model. Advertisement is down in general, with classified advertising particularly hard hit as consumers continue to move to free online sources. Moreover, media organizations are increasingly controlled by profit-driven, publicly traded corporations, rather than locally owned family companies. David Simon, a well-known reporter with the *Baltimore Sun* from 1982 to 1995, put it this way: "What do newspaper executives in Los Angeles or Chicago care whether or not readers in Baltimore have a better newspaper, especially when you can make more putting out a mediocre paper than a worthy one?"[21] Quite simply, profit-driven news organizations are reluctant to invest in the newsroom, especially during difficult economic times.[22] Even before the economic crisis that began in 2008, these corporations were experiencing a sharp decline in their revenue, as readership and advertising revenue began to tank.

A longtime journalist, Bob Wyse, reminds us that the United States used to be a nation of newspaper readers, but no longer. Wyse writes that "[i]n 1960 four out of five households read a daily paper. In 2005 that figure was one in two." He goes on to point out that "while the American population has risen, news circulation has fallen from 62 million in 1990 to 54 million in 2005."[23] The recent recession has dramatically accelerated a media transition that Wyse and others were reporting in 2005.

Early in 2009, the *Christian Science Monitor*, which has conducted high-quality print journalism for over a hundred years, announced that it was abandoning its daily print versions to focus its dwindling resources on its Internet presence. A month later, the *Seattle Post-Intelligencer*, in business for 146 years, announced that it too was abandoning its print edition and releasing the bulk of its staff. At the same time, the *Rocky Mountain News*, a 149-year-old news organization, announced that it was shuttering its entire news operation, Internet site and all. While many news organizations are increasing their online presence without entirely cutting their print editions, to date online revenue for major news organizations has failed to keep up with losses in its traditional news products.[24] The Project for Excellence in Journalism explains, "[M]ore and more it appears the biggest problem facing traditional media has less to do with where people get information than how to pay for it—the emerging reality is that advertising isn't migrating online with the consumer."[25]

David Simon put it this way: "High-end journalism is dying in America and unless a new economic model is achieved, it will not be reborn on the web or anywhere else."[26] It is not that the web is replacing print media; it is killing it. Simon summarizes the problem:

The internet is a marvelous tool and clearly it is the information delivery system of our future, but this far it does not deliver much first-generation reporting. Instead, it leeches that reporting from mainstream news publications, whereupon aggregating websites and bloggers contribute little more than repetition, commentary, and froth. Meanwhile, readers acquire news from the aggregators and abandon its point of origin—namely the newspapers themselves. In short, the parasite is slowly killing the host.[27]

Without a reliable source of advertising revenue, the markets are reacting to the long-term future of print media. Stock prices of newspapers fell 20 percent in 2006, 10 percent in 2007, and an astounding 42 percent in 2008.[28] Whether a news organization chooses to go the way of *The Monitor*, or to experiment with other business models, all print media outlets are aggressively trying to cut expenses faster then their revenues are falling. In 2008, the Project for Excellence in Journalism reported:

> More rounds of cutbacks in 2007 will be matched by even further scaling back in 2008. A firm number for job losses in 2007 is hard to gauge. We calculate the industry has lost a net of 3,000 print jobs from 2000 through 2006. With all appropriate caveats, we estimate as a reasonable guess for 2007 that somewhere in the neighborhood of 1,000 to 1,500 print jobs will be lost, with a gain of perhaps half that number added to the online workforce.[29]

The findings of Pew's *Journalists Survey 2008*, sponsored by the Pew Research Center for the People and the Press, reflects the dismal state of print journalism today.[30] The survey found that financial concerns overshadow other concerns of reporters. In an open-ended question, 55 percent of journalists at national news organizations identified financial concerns as the most important problem facing journalism, which is up from 30 percent in 2004. Among these same journalists, 62 percent responded that journalism is going in the wrong direction. Among local print journalists surveyed, 82 percent said that staffs at their news organizations have decreased over the past three years; 69 percent of national print journalists reported cuts; and 52 percent of Internet journalists also reported downsizing.

The bottom line is that "fewer people are being asked to do more," and they are feeling the pressure.[31] But it is not just that size matters (i.e., less resources lead to less coverage); it is also that the pressure to attract readers in an ever-shrinking media market can change the very nature of news coverage. The rapid decline in print journalism changes the logic of what is and is not news. The Pew Research Center makes this point:

A growing proportion of journalists believe that increased bottom-line pressure is not just changing the ways things get done in newsrooms. In addition, it is *hurting* the quality of news coverage. Roughly two-thirds of internet (69%), national and local journalists (68% each) say that increased bottom-line pressure is seriously hurting the quality of news coverage, rather than just changing the way news organizations operate.[32]

With growing numbers of journalists being bought out, laid off, furloughed, or having their beat consolidated with other beats, it is not surprising that the Pew study finds that journalists are highly critical of the way news organizations are covering the news. Eighty-two percent of those surveyed from national news organizations complained that too much news is being cut. Large majorities of journalists across the different news categories believe that too little attention is given to complex issues. And a majority of journalists believe that news outlets are now blurring the line between reporting and commentary.

The unprecedented pressures that the news providers currently face have far-reaching implications for our society. The wholesale cuts to newsrooms require that news organizations make hard decisions, which often mean trimming or eliminate "nonessential" elements of their programming. Commenting on the issue, Bob Lewis, a reporter for the Associated Press, recalls, "It's not just the bodies that are gone—it's the institutional memory and knowledge."[33] Marc Fisher of the *Washington Post* warns, "A combination of media revolution and economic collapse is dismantling our news infrastructure." Fisher goes on to explain that paid "lobbyists are getting the news they need. The voters, not so much."[34]

The State of Environmental Journalism

While regular coverage of environmental news began in the 1960s, environmental journalism did not come into its own until the late 1980s and early

Table 3.1   Large Majorities of Journalists Agree That Quality News Coverage Is on the Decline

	Type of Journalist		
	National	Local	Internet
Scope of news coverage cut too much	82%	73%	85%
Too little attention to complex issues	78%	83%	81%
Blurring of reporting and commentary	64%	54%	60%

Source: Adapted by the author from the Pew Research Center's *Journalists Survey 2008*.

1990s.[35] By this time the straightforward, event-driven reporting that domi-nated early environmental news coverage gave way to a more sophisticated and nuanced brand of reporting.[36] Sharon Friedman of Lehigh University, who has studied the thirty-year evolution of environmental news coverage, explains:

> The 1990s became the decade that environmental journalism as practiced by full-time specialty reporters grew into its shoes, becoming more sophisticated with the help of the Internet and a professional organization, the Society of Environmental Journalists. The field also matured as stories changed from relatively simple event-driven pollution stories to those of far greater scope and complexity such as land use management, global warming, resource conservation, and bio-technology.[37]

During this period two Pulitzer Prizes were awarded for environmental sto-ries, and the major networks were dedicating hundreds of minutes to envi-ronmental news per year. In 1989 alone, ABC, CBS, and NBC spent 774 minutes of airtime on environmental stories. By the year 2000 that number would fall to 280 minutes.[38]

It seems that environmental news coverage hinges more on the state of the economy, more specifically the state of the print news industry, than on the state of the world. Environmental journalism is the media equivalent of the red-headed stepchild—when times get tough and hard choices have to be made, we know which child is going have their college fund raided. When media budgets are slashed and tough decisions are made in the newsroom, we know which beat is going to be cut first, and times have never been tougher in the print media business than they are right now.

The rapid decline that has hit print media is having a disturbing impact on environmental news coverage. While media outlets can still be counted on to cover a major environmental accident or natural disaster, their ability to provide continued coverage of complex environmental matters is increas-ingly coming into question. Faced with an ever-shrinking readership and a corresponding loss in advertisement revenue, news organizations have shrunk the environmental news hole (the amount of space allocated to environmen-tal coverage), cut back the size of their environmental teams, and in some cases entirely eliminated their environmental units.

In the winter of 2008, CNN shocked media watchers when it announced its plans to fire its entire science, technology, and environment unit, includ-ing award-winning journalists Miles O'Brien and Peter Dykstra. The announcement was followed by a scathing letter from the presidents of the

Council for the Advancement of Science Writing, National Association of Science Writers, Society of Environmental Journalists, and World Federation of Science Journalists in which they scolded CNN for "wielding this ax" and for the loss of an "experienced and highly regarded group of science journalists at a time when science coverage could not be more important in our national and international discourse."[39]

Liz Shogen, who covered the environmental beat for the *Los Angeles Times* for four years before taking a job as an environmental reporter for National Public Radio in 2004, describes the change:

> The L.A. Times gave me lots of time to work on stories. I was able to spend months sniffing around the agencies and tromping through places like the coal fields of West Virginia and eastern Wyoming's coal methane boom . . . [but] The L.A. Times Washington bureau where I did those stories is now closed.[40]

Seth Borenstein, a science and environment writer for the Associated Press, puts it this way:

> [Y]ou've got a shrinking staff, there are fewer of you, you've got to do more work, so you're not going to get as much time to write . . . [in the past] I got to do stories about reduced environmental enforcement, reduced superfund work . . . those are things you can do when you have a little more time.[41]

Closer to home, the state of news reporting is no better. In January 2009, Capital Gazette Communications, publisher of *The Capital*, a regional daily newspaper in Annapolis with a strong reputation for its environmental reporting, announced that it was laying off 111 full-time and part-time employees. The cuts came in the wake of twenty-five voluntary buyouts the company made the previous year. While it is not yet clear what the cuts will mean for environmental news coverage at *The Capital*, what is obvious is that the remaining reporters, including *The Capital*'s lone environmental reporter, will be asked to perform more services with fewer resources. One month after *The Capital* announced its cuts, the *Baltimore Examiner* produced its last newspaper, citing slower than expected advertising sales as the reason for releasing its entire staff of ninety people.

The decline in environmental news has had a tangible impact on the coverage of the Chesapeake Bay. Not long ago the *Baltimore Sun* was hailed as the region's leader in environmental print journalism and enjoyed a healthy stable of three outstanding environmental reporters (Tom Pelton, Tim Wheeler, and Rona Kobell) and a popular environmental columnist (Tom

Horton). But in the last five years the *Sun*'s environmental team has been slashed (Tom Pelton left the *Sun* to take a job with the nonprofit Chesapeake Bay Foundation; Rona Kobell departed to enter a graduate school program at the University of Michigan; Tom Horton retired and his popular column was canceled). Tim Wheeler, one of the nation's top environmental reporters, remains at the *Sun* as its only full-time environmental reporter. And the problems at the *Sun* are in no way unique. Laurence Latane, who covered the Chesapeake Bay beat for twenty years with the *Richmond Times-Dispatch*, recently left the paper, leaving Rex Springston as the *Dispatch*'s sole environmental reporter.

The decline of environmental journalism means more than simply losing environmental positions. Karl Blankenship, himself a longtime reporter for the nonprofit *Bay Journal*, has studied the issue. Blankenship found that the space available to the remaining journalists has shrunk. Blankenship explains, "[S]ome reporters are simply skipping stories because they cannot cover them in 400 words,"[42] while others, like Tim Wheeler, are increasingly placing important news stories on their blogs, stories that earlier would have made the print edition. While online news sources are often an excellent source of information, they are generally read by a relatively small group of news seekers, people who already have an interest or concern about the topic. Blogs generally do little to raise awareness among the mass of people for whom environmental conditions are a secondary concern.

He also found that news organizations, magazines in particular, are increasingly relying on freelance reporters to write stories that were once written by their own staff writers. Another consequence is that local and regional papers are increasingly relying on stories from wire services to cover "their" environmental beat. Blankenship points out that since television, radio, and Internet news organizations feed off the reporting of the print journalists, the loss of coverage by print journalists has a ripple effect throughout the entire news environment. The net result is fewer reporters, with fewer resources, competing for less space, and ultimately a public that is less aware about the pressing environmental issues of the day.

In the 1995 edition of *The Reporter's Environmental Handbook*, published at a time when print media was relatively healthy, the authors explained, "Big risks deserve big news stories, especially if the proper authorities are ignoring them. Small risks deserve small stories, or no stories at all." According the *Environmental Handbook*, the trick to environmental journalism was simply determining which stories addressed high-risk issues and which did not.[43] But since 1995, the basic questions that environmental reporters face when considering their stories have changed.

Today their calculations are less about calculating "risk" then they are about calculating readership and how an editor might view the market for a story. In the current economic climate, risk is fine if it helps sell papers, but if the risk is too complex to grab the reader's attention or too divisive to appeal to the base audience, a reporter might be better off considering a different topic or transforming the story into a human interest story that is likely to have more widespread appeal. Stories about the female astronaut in diapers who drove from Houston to Orlando to confront her romantic rival trump stories about the Mars Polar Lander; stories about polar bears drowning or whales trapped in the ice; stories about the tragic death of Steve Irwin (the much-watched crocodile hunter); replace stories about the decline of natural resources around the globe.[44]

In the current economic context it is increasingly important to understand the pressures that environmental journalists face as they struggle to protect their careers and cover the green beat. Moreover, it has never been more important to understand how these professional pressures might color environmental news and what it might mean for life within the political dead zone.

Understanding the Environmental Beat

While no two news beats are the same (e.g., business news beat, crime beat, political beat), the environmental beat is perhaps the most challenging of them all. For the crime reporter, a weekend murder is the story—who, what, where, when, and why, followed by a few annual crime statistics if space allows. The conflict is clear and the story is obvious. The business reporter has the stock market to watch and a steady flow of economic reports to cover. The sports reporter has the "big game" to report, and the political reporter has an endless supply of breaking news regarding campaigns and legislative battles, not to mention the occasional juicy scandal.

But environmental issues are particularly difficult to cover from a news perspective, as they often require a level of technical or scientific understanding that is not widespread within the general public, and they tend to address problems that have existed for extended periods of time or that involve long-term trends that are difficult to observe at any given moment. Getting the public to care about and understand environmental issues is no small task.

Moreover, environmental stories place a tremendous burden on the environmental news reporter, who must possess knowledge of environmental law, economics, ethics, science, and politics to get the story right. No other beat covers the scope and complexity of the issues covered by the environmental news reporter.

On a day-to-day basis, it is not at all clear how a reporter should cover a fifty-year decline of an ecosystem, or a one-degree increase in global temperatures over a fifty-year period of time, or an incremental loss in biodiversity, or the environmental consequences of the nation's energy dependence. In short, for environmental journalists identifying *the* story of the day or week is often a difficult challenge. One observer explains the unique nature of environmental coverage this way: environmental issues are "more subtle, more technical, and more chronic than acute, though no less real and significant."[45] The primary difference between the environmental beat and other beats is that reporters in other beats can "cover" the news. In contrast, environmental reporters are often called on to "unearth" the news.

Sometimes a breaking event will drive environmental coverage for a period of time (e.g., the Exxon-Valdez oil spill, the Bhopal chemical accident, the Cuyahoga River catching on fire, the Three Mile Island nuclear crisis, the Chernobyl nuclear disaster, the Tennessee Valley Authority fly ash spill), or a member of the scientific community will release the findings of an important new study, or a major green initiative will be proposed by the White House or a state's governor. For the most part, however, environmental journalists have far greater leeway in determining what is and is not news. It is this leeway that makes environmental news unique and that gives environment reporting its central role in the policy process.

The scope and complexity of environmental issues tend to give environmental reporters greater flexibility when choosing topics (i.e., what to cover and what not to cover), but this same complexity, coupled with increased competition for space within the ever-shrinking daily paper, tends to dictate the nature of the stories (i.e., how reporters frame them). In other words, environmental reporters are generally free to cover what they want, but they are not free to cover it how they want—environmental journalists are required to make their stories "newsworthy" (i.e., marketable) to the general public. The larger issue of climate change might be framed as a sensationalized piece about a celebrity's carbon footprint or a stylized piece about ways to celebrate a carbon-neutral Valentine's Day. The hundred-year decline to the Chesapeake Bay might become a story about transgender fish in the

Potomac or a story about a prominent public official violating a specific environmental law.

Have editorial pressures within the hypercompetitive news market (i.e., the pressure to produce stories that will help sell papers and generate advertising revenue), coupled with the career goals of individual journalists, affected the way environmental news is covered? And if so, has the increased pressure on environmental journalists to justify their very existence and the substantial discretion exercised by environmental reporters when choosing stories led journalists to shy away from tackling the long-term and often technical environmental questions in favor of more focused stories related to isolated events, specific conflicts, personalities, and human interest topics? In short, have increased market pressures led to sensationalizing environmental news that leaves the general public with nebulous concerns about the environment but little actual knowledge of environmental matters?

To explore these issues, we first address the professional goals of journalists. In the second section, we explore how the professional goals of journalists influence their actions (i.e., how what journalists want influences what they do). Here we take a look at the strategies and tactics that environmental journalists employ in pursuit of their professional goals. Lastly, we consider how editors' views of their readers and their perceptions might influence the way reporters pursue their goals and ultimately the way that they cover environmental news (i.e., how perceptions of news consumers influence the news products that media outlets produce).[46]

Goals of the Environmental Reporter

It would be nice if all journalists were tireless servants of the public good, willing to make considerable professional and personal sacrifices in order to fulfill their civic responsibility to inform the public. But this expectation is no more realistic than expecting all politicians to behave selflessly for the public good, or to expect all business leaders to welcome higher taxes for the sake of the public good, or any other group of professionals to make sacrifices for the sake of others. Like other professionals participating in a free-market economy, journalists pursue their individual professional objectives with the hope that taking actions to advance their careers will also help promote the public good. While an altruistic drive might have motivated an undergraduate to pursue a career in journalism, it does little to sustain them throughout their career.

Journalism has always been a highly competitive industry, with unrelenting deadlines, unforgiving editors, and long hours. An aspiring young reporter might have started honing his or her skills in college or even in high school, writing for the school paper. Once out of college, an entry-level position might consist of writing obituaries for a local or regional paper. As one seasoned journalist once explained, there is nothing like writing obituaries to hone a young reporter's eye for detail, as every mistake will be noticed by the families and friends of the deceased.[47] Over time a cub reporter might get a chance to serve on one of the paper's less appealing beats, such as the local homicide beat or local sports beat. If they succeed with these assignments, a reporter may rise in the ranks, covering issues of greater importance and ultimately finding themselves with opportunities to reach a larger audience. But for every reporter writing on subjects of their choice, for the paper of their dreams, there are countless other reporters toiling up the ranks. For the most part, news is written by people who would rather be covering something else or working for a different news organization, and understanding the desires and goals of reporters is the key to understanding why reporters cover the news the way that they do.

Job Security

The first general goal of all professionals, environmental reporters included, is to establish *job security* within their existing institution (i.e., the desire to perform their job in such a way that they are unlikely to be demoted or fired in the future).[48] In the past, when print media was on a healthier financial footing and environmental reporting was a growing beat, this concern was relatively minor. But with the steady decline of print media, this most basic concern has risen in importance among environmental reporters. Without job security, reporters are ill-positioned to increase their institutional clout or to seek professional advancement from external sources. Job security is to reporters what reelection is to elected officials—*the* essential goal upon which all others rest. And in the current news environment no one's job is entirely secure, least of all the environmental reporter's.

Institutional Clout

The second goal of the environmental reporter is to increase their *institutional clout* (institutional clout is a reporter's professional status within their news organization). "Institutional clout" differs depending on the news organization. At a national paper it might mean making the move from the metro section to the paper's national section. It might mean expanding one's beat from a specific issue like weather-related stories to a broader umbrella of environmental concerns (e.g., covering the Florida Everglades restoration process or covering climate change). It might also mean moving from the environmental beat altogether (which generally provides less job security and fewer opportunities for advancement than other beats) to a more prestigious beat, like the political beat. It could also mean moving to a leadership position with the paper, such as a bureau chief or editor.

Advancement

The third general goal of the environmental reporter is to seek *advancement* (i.e., the desire to seek professional advancement from outside their current employer). Except for the very top echelon of plum positions at national papers and national magazines, most print reporters seek opportunities for advancement. A local reporter might seek a position at a regional paper; a reporter at the regional paper might desire a position at a national publication. And even reporters at national publications might seek publication opportunities that can further their careers, such as lucrative book deals or opportunities to host radio or television programs.

While none of the goals of the environmental reporter mentioned here are unique to environmental journalism or even journalism for that matter, the unique nature of environmental journalism does have interesting consequences for the environmental reporter as they pursue these general goals. With environmental news viewed as one of the least essential aspects of the news organization, pursuing even the most basic goal of job security—never mind increased clout or advancement—can become problematic for the environmental reporter. In the current context, the environmental beat remains at risk of being cut or eliminated. While the threat is greatest at local and regional papers, even the largest news organizations have seen their environmental reporting teams slashed in recent years or seen positions go vacant after an established environmental reporter leaves the beat. It is in this context, with their most basic professional goals in question, that most environmental reporters conduct their work. Some choose to abandon the environmental beat for more secure positions, where upward mobility is more likely, while others hope to buck the odds and make a career out of environmental reporting. But in all cases, it is likely that the professional pressures mentioned here color the way environmental reporters cover the news.

The Elements of Career Success
for Environmental Journalists

Reporters generally pursue a three-pronged strategy toward their broad professional goals. The elements outlined here are keys to obtaining the general goals mentioned in the previous section. Successfully achieving the specific objectives discussed here does not guarantee professional success for the environmental reporter, but missing one or more of the objectives does assure professional problems.

Editorial Trust

For most reporters, the key ingredient for professional success is winning *editorial trust* (the trust of their immediate supervisor, the editor). Editors ultimately decide what stories are cut from the paper and what stories will be trimmed. Likewise, it is the all-important editor who decides when a story will run and where it will be placed within the paper. With the full support and trust of their editor, an environmental reporter can run the types of stories that can increase their job security, amplify their clout, and ultimately provide them with career opportunities outside of their organization. But without editorial trust, the journalist risks falling into a type of editorial hell—where constant battles for space and placement within the paper dominate the reporter's time and energy.

Professional Reputation

Another key to achieving professional success is cultivating one's *professional reputation* (the reporter's reputation among other reporters and media insiders). Within the environmental beat only a small number of reporters are typically covering a specific issue. For example, in the mid-Atlantic region of the United States there are fewer than a dozen print journalists who cover the Chesapeake Bay on a regular basis. These reporters (and their editors) typically read each others' work, they know who scooped who on a certain story, and who won a spot on the coveted front page. They also know who had their stories cut, who was passed over for an open position at the national paper, a position for which several of them probably applied, and who won a prestigious award. David Simon recalls the power of reputation:

> The self-gratification of my profession does not come, you see, from covering a city and covering it well, from explaining an increasingly complex and interconnected world to citizens, from holding basic institutions accountable on a daily basis. It comes from someone handing you a plaque and taking your picture.[49]

Over time a hierarchy of reputation is established among the environmental reporters covering a specific beat. The reporters may be friendly and supportive of each other, but make no mistake: they are all in competition.

Public Readership

A third major element of success for the environmental reporter is developing a dedicated *public readership*. While few people subscribe to a particular paper because of the work of a single reporter, many environmental reporters do in fact develop a dedicated followership over time. For example, Tom Horton, who was hired as the *Baltimore Sun's* first full-time environmental reporter in 1974 and worked for the *Sun* as a reporter then a columnist until he retired in 2006, was such a person. Many people in the watershed learned about the Bay and its problems through his weekly column, *On the Bay*. Horton's followership, as well as his professional reputation and the trust that he enjoyed at the *Sun*, translated into unprecedented flexibility as a reporter. Looking back on his years with the *Sun*, Horton explained the situation this way: "they left me alone, I decided who I wanted to talk to and what I wanted to write . . . I do not know who would be supported by their paper today to travel around the Bay and do the type of reporting I did."

The elements for achieving professional goals outlined here should not be seen as mutually exclusive. As Horton's case suggests, achieving success in one area inevitably increases the reporter's position in the other areas. Developing a large readership helps develop editorial trust (as editors are concerned with selling papers and market share) and helps to develop a professional reputation in the field. Moreover, winning an award for journalism (a sign of one's professional reputation) would go a long way in securing editorial trust and might even help boost readership. Likewise, a reporter who has won the support of the paper's editorial staff is far more likely to earn a place on the paper's front page or to be given a column, which in turn increases the journalist's reputation and public readership. Each of these factors has a direct impact on one's job security, institutional clout, and potential for external professional advancement.

While each factor influences the behavior of reporters, on a day-to-day basis editorial approval is the greatest concern for reporters. In competition for space and positioning within a paper, editors will ultimately determine which stories win and which lose. Whether the issue is politics, business, entertainment, or the environment, no story goes to print without editorial approval and no reporter is long for a publication without the full support of their editorial staff. The reporter's first reader is always the editor.

How Editors View Their Readers

In order to understand how reporters' career goals can be translated in specific tactics that color their reporting, it is important to first understand how editors view their readers. Editors live in the hinter-world of journalism, with one foot in the world of the reporter (seeking the news) and another foot firmly planted in the world of business (seeking readers). Norman Miller, whose book addresses the media's role in the environmental policy making process, explains the situation this way: "At the core of the media's mission are two obligations: to inform their readers and viewers of events and circumstances . . . and to earn a profit."[50] Editors are forced to bridge the gap between the market and the issue; they are the ones who deal with economic realities of the publishing world by selling stories in the marketplace of ideas. For the editor, readers (i.e., news consumers) can be classified into three broad categories.

Confused and Concerned

Given the complex nature of most environmental issues, the bulk of newspaper readers fall into the category of *confused and concerned* (readers with a low level of knowledge regarding the environment but a general concern regarding environmental conditions). Consequently, the bulk of environmental reporting is directed at this group. Members of this group are worried about environmental conditions but lack sufficient information to fully understand the problems at hand and lack sufficient interest in the topic to become fully informed. Recent studies have shown that Americans lack basic science knowledge, with half of Americans unable to identify how long it takes the earth to orbit the sun.[51] Members of this group might be concerned about global warming in general but do not understand why it is happening or how their decisions influence climate change. Or they might be concerned about the state of the Bay; they might even have a "Save the Bay" bumper sticker on their car or SUV, but ask them to explain how nutrients influence the Bay and they are unlikely to have much to say. They include the majority of Americans who believe that environmental conditions are getting worse[52] and who are generally willing to do something to help the environment, but they are not quite sure what exactly that something is.

With the public generally lacking a basic scientific foundation upon which to make judgments, environmental journalists make use of "hooks" to interest their audience.[53] To attract attention from this group, reporters are asked to identify novelty, conflict, human interest twists, intriguing narratives, local importance, celebrity connections, human health angles, and anything else that might make the story interesting to the amorphous "general public."[54] Pictures become substitutes for words, as reporters and editors try any emotional hook to appeal to this group. As one prominent environmental journalist explained, write a story about an exotic species with a strange scientific name (*channa argus*) that poses no real risk to humans and the story will go nowhere. But write a story about the "snake-head fish" and describe it in such a way that it sounds like it can "crawl on the land and eat your cat" and suddenly your story is the talk of the town.[55] The name alone, "snake-head," warrants attention. Ultimately, the snake-head fish story, along with its startling images, was irresistible because it was novel, it focused on a perceived threat, and it was a local issue to the residents of the Chesapeake Bay region. Never mind the fact that the animal posed very little risk to the Bay, as it can only live in freshwater, and the fact that *channa argus* is mostly a threat to the freshwater bass, which themselves are not native to the Potomac.

Informed and Interested
Readers with a deep interest and understanding of environmental matters (*informed and interested*) are not entirely ignored by environmental journalism, but editors know that this minority group can be counted on to read environmental news. Unlike the confused and concerned group who are passive news consumers, the informed and interested readers are active news seekers. The informed and interested readers are of concern to environmental journalists in that they will point out mistakes or omissions in environmental news coverage, which can tarnish a journalist's reputation and cause a reporter to lose the trust of the paper's editorial staff. Tom Horton recalls that he once wrote a story about the apparent connection between the use of herbicides (common weed killers sold at garden stores) and the decline of the Bay grasses. The only problem was that connection was false, a point that was quickly pointed out to the reporter and his editor.[56] An honest mistake now and again, like this one, will not end a reporter's career, but make a habit of getting the story wrong and editors will take note. Appealing to the informed and interested readers is less about career advancement for an environmental reporter than it is about protecting job security.

Uninterested
Those with no interest in the subject (*uninterested*) are essentially written off, as they are unlikely to read environmental news and consequently can do little to enhance or harm a journalist's career, though they might read the occasional story about a snake-head fish. It is worth noting that there is a fourth group, too small to warrant its own separate category, but certainly well known to seasoned environmental reporters. For lack of a better word,

one senior reporter referred to them as "the crazies." Reporters and editors alike know that no matter how they cover a story, no matter how thorough their reporting, there is a small vocal minority within the environmental community that will find fault with a story. Since this group can be relied on to read the news and is generally impossible to satisfy, they are essentially treated the same way as the "uninterested"; they too are ignored.

The net result is that editors, and in turn reporters, focus their attention on attracting readers with moderate or low interest in the topic, a group that comprises the bulk of actual and latent newspaper readers, while avoiding making glaring mistakes or omissions. Those with no interest in the topic and the crazies are ignored by the print media. The problem, of course, is that the types of stories that appeal to the confused and concerned group are not the types of stories that actually educate readers. Novelty, conflict, human interest twists, intriguing narratives, local importance, celebrity connections, and human health angles can cause concern, maybe even raise awareness, but they often lack the context and background that would be necessary for readers to understand environmental issues. The problem is not simply that gusto is added to make the "story" marketable; the problem is that gusto becomes an acceptable substitute for actual news reporting. Norman Miller explains:

> It was not so very long ago that what appeared under headlines in the newspaper were routinely called "articles," and their first paragraph just as routinely answered "the five Ws—who, what, where, when, and why." Today, they are almost always called "stories," and, accordingly, often begin anecdotally, with the introduction of particular people in a situation emblematic of the larger one that is the main subject of the piece . . . Its principal value is to take what the readers may regard as dry and academic and make it into a mini-drama that they may someday find themselves involved in.[57]

Mini-dramas might be entertaining, but they are no way to learn about the most pressing issues of our time. As print media continues to fall, the competition for the confused and concerned continues to grow, adding pressure to write stories that appeal to this group. As figure 3.1 suggests, the system is a closed loop of mediocrity in which mediocre reporting fosters a mediocre level of public understanding, which in turn drives the demand for mediocre reporting. Environmental reporters, under greater and greater pressure to justify their existence, translate this pressure into what editors demand and the general public wants—emotional stories that cause concern but that do little to direct that concern in any meaningful direction.

Societal
Consequence

Sensationalizing environmental news leaves
the general public with nebulous concerns about
the environment, but little actual knowledge of
environmental matters (environmental
reporting increases the ranks of the
confused and concerned)

News
Outcome

Environmental news tend to identify conflict,
human interest twists, intriguing narratives,
or relate the stories to the readers' circumstances

Tactics

Appeal to the "confused and concerned" without
alienating the "informed and interested"

Elements of
Career Success

Professional
Goals

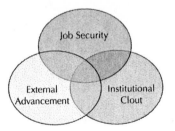

Figure 3.1

Conclusion

As discussed in the previous chapter, one reason markets fail (whether they are economic markets or the political marketplace of ideas) is because the general public lacks the information necessary to make informed decisions. It is not just that heightened competition within print media is leading to poor reporting; it is that poor reporting leads to a news climate in which the political dead zone can flourish. Consumers are left unaware of the environmental price of the lifestyles they pursue and the public policies that they tolerate. Some consumers might be willing to pay extra for agricultural products that were produced in an environmentally friendly manner. But lacking information about the environmental harm caused by outdated agricultural practices and no firsthand knowledge of modern corporate agricultural practices, consumers base their purchasing decisions on other factors—more often than not, price. The outcome is a market advantage to those producers who have done the least to control their unwanted by-products and a political system that provides few pressures on elected officials to correct these market failures.

Lacking sufficient information to connect the state of the environment with actions and inactions of policy makers, citizens are easily duped by political actors. All elected officials report a concern for the environment, even those with the most anti-environmental voting records, and take credit for collaborative environmental programs. Occasionally a news reporter has the courage and the resources necessary to challenge the political spin, but by and large they miss the big-picture story in pursuit of a more amusing and marketable narrative. The public is left entertained, journalists strive to reach their professional markers, politicians take credit for policies that they know are inadequate, polluters remain underregulated, and ecosystems like the Bay steadily decline—welcome to the political dead zone.

↙

CHAPTER FOUR

Fighting for the Bay

Environmental Advocacy in the Dead Zone

The good, the illuminated, sit apart from the rest, censuring their dullness and vices, as if they thought that by sitting very grand in their chairs, the very brokers, attorneys, and congressmen would see the error of their ways, and flock to them. But the good and wise must learn to act, and carry salvation to the combatants and demagogues in the dusty area below.

—Ralph Waldo Emerson (1843)[1]

In the summer months, when nutrient pollution causes oxygen levels in the Bay to plummet, you can find swollen dead fish, sometimes by the tens of thousands, floating on the surface of the Bay, a sure sign that the dead zone has returned. The tenacious blue crab, never willing to die without a fight, has a unique strategy for avoiding the oxygen-starved waters; at times they will actually leave the Bay's polluted waters and congregate on the shore or along pilings. The crabs come on land in a desperate attempt for survival in a phenomenon the Chesapeake Bay watermen call a "crab jubilee."

This chapter is reserved for the tenacious advocates of the Bay who are engaged in their own "advocacy jubilee." They are the good folks who have struggled within the political dead zone in an uphill effort to achieve sensible environmental policies for the Bay. While the entries listed here represent only a tiny fraction of the thousands of people who have worked to promote environmental policy in the Chesapeake Bay region, they do represent a broad spectrum of the efforts, from light green to dark green.

The first entry is written by Anne Pearson and represents an innovative light green effort to promote wise land use policies. The second entry, "The Inside Game," by former Maryland state senator Gerald Winegrad, recalls the difficulties he faced when trying to promote his green policies within the Maryland State Senate. The third entry, by Tyla Matteson and Glen Besa, reveals a more dark green approach to environmental protection: their effort to save the Mattaponi River. And the final case study, thoroughly dark green in nature, is written by Mike Shay and recalls his decade-long effort to preserve open spaces along the Bay. The chapter ends with concluding remarks by the dean of the Bay advocacy, Bernie Fowler.

What the entries have in common is that they are firsthand accounts from those who have toiled on the front lines of environmental advocacy. They illustrate the difficulties that sincere advocates face when they are forced to work within a political system that is better designed to defuse their energy than it is to harness it. They also reveal law advocates make use of the media in their pursuit of environmental action. Like the indomitable blue crab who struggles for survival in the Bay's degraded waters, these advocates work against tremendous odds to locate the political oxygen (political will) that enables their efforts to succeed. They do not always win, but they never give up without a good fight.

In Defense of Sacred Places

Guest entry by Anne Pearson

Having tried my hand in theatre, public relations, and real estate, I made a bold decision in the summer of 1976, one that would change the course of my life—I sold my home in Annapolis and moved my family to the wilderness of Fox Point in Pembroke, Maine. For the next eight years I lived on a seventy-five-acre wooded peninsula, where my children and I worked and studied together, building a self-sufficient life centered on simplicity. We lived without power, telephone, or plumbing. Over time we built an addition to our one-room log cabin, cleared land, and planted and harvested vegetables. For income I designed and hand-knit sweaters for sale in specialty shops.

We eventually left the serenity of the Maine wilderness with the hope of sharing with others the many lessons we had learned; my son and daughter left to pursue their own lives, and I found my way back to the town of Annapolis, Maryland. The city seemed busier, sprawling beyond its traditional creek boundaries, but it was still recognizably Annapolis with its historic buildings and maritime roots. What I brought back with me, and what my children took with them, was a profound sense of "belonging to the earth." It was in this spirit that in May 1994, I established the Alliance for Sustainable Communities.

I designed the nonprofit to promote innovative examples of sustainable policy and to motivate partnerships between existing organizations, citizens, and government officials. The overarching goal was to promote sound environmental policies that provide a base for economic health and social well-being. The idea was to help promote a green infrastructure that respects and preserves natural functions; that protects essential human needs; that assigns the true value to clean air, clean water, and good earth for growing food; and that inspires the heart and spirit and guides the mind. Stated differently, the goal was to help protect the natural landscape from fragmentation and sprawl development, which I believe devours the landscape and destroys its meaning and function.

While developing community planning ideas, I discovered the work of a University of California professor, Randolph Hester, and I was immediately taken by his approach. Hester was not only teaching community-based planning, but he and his wife, Marcia McNally, were taking their ideas to the public, offering two-day workshops on community planning. Hester calls the process he originated "sociologically based planning." He developed the approach after being hired to craft and develop a plan for the town of Manteo, North Carolina, only to find that the citizens of Manteo strongly objected to his vision for their community. To address their concerns, Hester called on his opponents, one by one, and asked them what they valued most in their community. From this dialogue, essentially asking community members what they most want to preserve and enhance, Hester developed his sociologically based planning approach.

Based on the input of the citizens of Manteo, Hester rewrote the plan, with greater attention given to the importance of reviving historic waterfront trades in a focused town center and preserving a natural forest-wetland boundary for the town. The new plan awakened the energy and imagination of the community. With his most outspoken critics now the plan's strongest supporters, the citizens of Manteo volunteered their time and resources to realize their combined vision. The result was an unqualified success, stimulating interest in boatbuilding, preserving the town's waterfront for the enjoyment of its residents and visitors, and in the process preserving the area's forests, marshes, and water quality.

Having been deeply disillusioned by the lack of vision and courage shown by local planners and policy makers in the Chesapeake Bay region, I hoped to replicate Dr. Hester's innovative approach in my area. Ultimately, I hoped that Hester's approach could begin a process that would reverse zoning and permitting decisions that all too often fragment the landscape and ignore the environment. I submitted a grant proposal to the Environmental Protection Agency's Chesapeake Bay Program. My proposal was straightforward; I would provide demonstration training sessions in Maryland, Virginia, and Pennsylvania that introduce planners and citizens to Randolph Hester's sociologically based community planning. In exchange, the Bay Program would provide the necessary funding to support the workshops and promote community-based planning for the Bay watershed.

Within weeks I learned that the grant request had been funded, and I immediately began working with planners in Pennsylvania, Virginia, and Maryland to select demonstration communities for the workshops. Dr. Hester and Marcia McNally agreed to help guide the workshops, and together we set out to replicate the success that Hester and McNally had experienced in Manteo. We hoped to challenge planners and citizens to work together to identify specific elements in the built and natural landscapes that are essential to the community's well-being. The essential point of the process was to teach local planners how to join with citizens to evoke the essence of places they cherish and to conceptualize that elusive element commonly referred to as "quality of life." Rather than impose a zoning plan on citizens, with fractured input from the public, the sociologically based process is designed to unify citizens and government officials, giving citizens the leading role in the community planning process.

In Virginia, we conducted our two-day mapping and discussion workshop in rural Rockbridge County. A geologist from Washington and Lee University opened the session by explaining the topography of the area, as well as the region's underlying soil formations. The information allowed the participants to understand the natural framework in which future development would occur. The enthusiasm expressed by the group for this kind of information led to requests for guided tours by the geologist, which he happily provided. Following the geologist, Dr. Hester presented his lecture, expressing the lessons from the Manteo experience and the foundations of sociologically based planning. The lecture was followed by a bus tour that allowed the workshop participants to explore "their place" and to identify distinctive places or qualities that hold special meaning for them and their community.

Later we identified these special places on maps of the county, including photos and explanations of why the places were selected. Each group described their findings to the entire assemblage. The findings were recorded by a facilitator, and all the information was collected and entered into a computer. The final outcome of the workshop was the creation of an inventory of special places that planners could use when judging the appropriateness of proposed developments. In effect, we had quantified what made the area special to the citizens and identified what the citizens did not want to lose to future development. Essentially we had identified areas that should be off-limits to development, sites that are "sacred" to the community's well-being, as well as areas that could be enhanced to attract future local businesses.

The results of the Virginia workshop were spectacular. People who attended the workshop reported that they thought they knew their county, but had seen it with new eyes. The workshop inspired Rockbridge County citizens to develop a new nonprofit, "Imagine Rockbridge," which committed itself to a two-year public engagement. During this time the group worked to integrate ideas put forth from representatives from the white-collar town of Lexington, the working-class town of Buena Vista, Washington and Lee University, the chamber of commerce, and the county planner's office. The group developed public support for an unprecedented long-term vision that is geared toward preserving and enhancing what they called their "heritage landscape."

In Pennsylvania, the results were similar. An aroused citizenry praised the challenging lecture, participated in the bus tour, contributed to the photos and mapping of essential places. They too were challenged to view their county with new eyes and to assess the real value of clear, cold streams, mountain vistas, and fields of corn edging the county roads. Local youth, working with the county planner, developed slide presentations, which they made throughout the county to continue the process of citizen and business engagement and to develop popular support for new zoning regulations to replace the strip malls and subdivisions that were beginning to replace the area's heritage patterns.

In both Virginia and Pennsylvania, participants wished to preserve a heritage landscape, where small towns cluster around homes and businesses. They desired to preserve the small-town feel in which towns are nestled in farmland, while forest vistas provide a feeling of sanctuary, and clear streams offer the rewards of fishing and boating to residents and visitors alike. They spoke resoundingly of the vital need for new development to follow patterns that honor historic land use, that preserve fertile farmland, and that sustain local watershed functions. In the words of one participant, "Throughout the weekend I had to step back and tell myself that this is for real! I couldn't believe this kind of concern and interest from the whole community was possible, especially in today's isolationist society." But the concern was real and measurable.

We found that the places people described generally fell into certain "categories of meaning": 1) places of shelter (places that people liked because they were historical, or held memories for their families, or demonstrated good design); 2) places of transportation (pleasant roadways that linked the places of shelter and connected the towns); 3) meeting places (places that held the community together); 4) places for making a living (economic centers that anchored the towns and provided employment opportunities); 5) vistas (places that gave people a feeling of unity with the larger landscape). While each category of place was unique, together the participants identified these places of meaning as "sacred" to the heritage and their community. They were more than places on a map; they were part of their collective identity, an identity that they wished to preserve.

The workshops created bonds among the participants and helped them understand the importance of "listening" to each other, of "hearing" each other, and of "naming" the places in the landscape that have archetypal meaning for the community. The workshop provided people with a rare opportunity to come to terms with their mutual need for "meaning" in the landscape. The identification of these meanings developed common ground among the participants. Moreover, the community-based planning allowed residents to identify their "sacred" places as a group, reinforcing community interaction and collective identity. It captured the energies of citizens who might otherwise have been frustrated by their lack of access to a process that developers and bureaucrats tend to dominate. Moreover, it provided a planning tool that can make an all-important difference in the permitting process, capturing the essence of "quality of life" in a way that can be defended.

Having successfully completed the training in the traditionally more conservative states of Pennsylvania and Virginia, I hoped for even greater results in my home state of Maryland. To increase the challenge of the workshop, we selected an area that was experiencing tremendous pressure from development and urban sprawling. Carroll County, a historically rural area, had more recently been overtaken by the ever-expanding Baltimore/Washington Metropolitan Area, a region plagued by wide roads that led from one commercial mall to another and that isolated neighborhoods and the area's historic essence. We wanted to see if residents in an area of sprawl could also identify sacred places, and if they could envision their built landscape at peace with its surroundings.

What we found was a community divided. In our meetings with the county planner and representatives of various local organizations, we quickly discovered a level of contention that we had not experienced at our previous sessions, and quite frankly, we had not anticipated at this workshop. One particularly vocal and effective group consisting of local landowners was steadfastly committed to defending "private property rights" and opposed the very concept of the workshop on the grounds that their farms and their lands might be deemed "sacred" places and that the designation might interfere with their development rights.

Despite the opposition from the group, we went ahead with our plans for the workshop. After several meetings with the local government officials, the county officials voted in favor of supporting the two-day workshop. News that the workshop was going forward outraged the property rights group. They quickly organized and wrote angry letters to the local press, called on their congressional representatives for assistance, and even went so far as to call me directly and insist that I stop the workshop.

I saw firsthand how easy it was for a group of this kind to kindle fear in the name of property rights and how willing political actors were to react to the fear. Just fourteen days before the workshop was scheduled to take place, my contact at the Chesapeake Bay Program contacted me with the dreaded news. The Bay Program, having approved the workshop idea, having seen the program succeed in Virginia and Pennsylvania, and having committed funding for the project in Maryland, maintained that the workshop could not go forward under the fractious circumstances. Their position was clear; I was told to cancel the workshop. While I do not agree with their decision, I do understand their fear. The Bay Program relies on federal funding for its survival, and conservatives within Congress could cut their funding if they believed the Bay Program officials were meddling in people's private rights.

The problem was, of course, that the citizens' associations and local elected officials who supported the idea of the workshop had already committed to the effort and pleaded with me not to let them down. I was deeply moved and sorely perplexed by the situation. I felt a moral obligation to support the people and groups who had earlier agreed to support the workshop, and I certainly did not want to allow an unreasonable minority faction within the community to derail the process, but on the other hand I could hardly afford to burn my bridges at the Bay Program. I discussed the problem with the Bay Program officials. I offered to engage in the workshop under my own banner, thus protecting the Bay Program from any responsibility for the outcome. I proposed that if we succeeded in bringing the opposing factions together and the workshop achieved its desired results, as it had elsewhere, the Bay Program could reimburse me for the $5,000 cost for the consultants. If the program failed, I would pay the consultants' fees myself.

Despite my best efforts, officials at the Bay Program forbade me from going forward under any circumstances. I have never felt so deeply anguished. In the end, I believed it was my obligation to the community to go forward with the workshop. The woman who had taken her family to the woods of Maine was not going to cave in to the unreasonable demands of property rights fanatics and their apologists, even if it meant losing access to future grants, which it most certainly would. After a week of sleepless nights and consultation with my most trusted friends, I made the only decision I felt was honorable. I agreed to hold the workshop under the auspice of my nonprofit and hoped that the results would not undermine my future as a grant-dependent nonprofit. For better or worse, the workshop was going forward as planned.

At first, the property rights group threatened to "swamp" the workshop. Their threats were palpable. However, the landowners' brazen bullying backfired, as it united the more moderate elements of the community who effectively told the group to behave themselves. The group eventually agreed to limit their numbers and to participate in a reasonable manner. As might be expected, tensions were high at the start of the workshop, as suspicion and doubt clouded the faces of the property rights representatives. They interrupted with mean-spirited questions. But as the work progressed, they melded into the group and eventually participated with enthusiasm, even designating their own farms as sacred places, something they had feared and objected to previously. By the end of the two-day session, several members of the group embraced me, thanked me for the workshop, and declared it was a great experience.

Being the eternal optimist, following the workshop, I presented our findings to the Chesapeake Bay Program and hoped they would welcome our results. I documented our success in defeating antagonism toward land use preservation. I showed that even when faced with serious differences of opinion, the exercises could create a sense of well-being and unity that bridges the barriers of understanding. Despite the success of the workshops, I was unable to reestablish a working relationship with the Chesapeake Bay Program for several years. Not only did I lose $5,000 by following my conscience, but I would not receive another Bay Program grant for more than six years, and the guide we had jointly produced for conducting such workshops in the future was never implemented by the Bay Program. My disappointment was impossible to measure. How in the world could the Bay Program address the decline of the Chesapeake Bay if they were unable to support a meaningful land use dialogue? The process taught me that real collaborative partnerships respect all opinions, but do not give veto power to extremists.

My disappointment aside, the experience taught many other valuable lessons. It taught me that citizens in this country want to preserve a heritage landscape, where small towns nestle in farmland and forest vistas provide a feeling of sanctuary. They want to be part of the government process that determines how their quality of life is protected. It taught me that there are planning processes that can guide new development in a manner that honors historic land uses, that preserves fertile farmland, and that sustains local watershed functions.

People can come together under evocative guidance and agree on how to protect the essentials of place, while at the same time allowing beneficial change to occur. When people are given the opportunity to truly consider the things in their community that they cherish, they develop profound new insights. A community that cherishes farmland begins to understand that they need to find ways to help local farmers continue to make a living. They begin to think about ways they can buy farm products directly, avoiding the middleman, and increasing the profit of their local farmers. They think about waste in a new way, considering how they can make things to sell from things they normally discarded. They consider ways to preserve the quality of the water in their streams. They think about ways of supporting each others' needs, working together.

In the end, despite our many challenges and setbacks, we showed that giving attention to community rights, rather than focusing exclusively on private property rights, we can empower a community and protect its heritage landscape for the benefit of future generations.

The Inside Game

Guest entry by Gerald W. Winegrad

My environmental advocacy began in earnest in 1969 after graduating from law school. I began my career as an environmental attorney for the National Wildlife Federation in Washington, DC. One of the earliest matters I worked on was assuring that the full panoply of air and water quality laws were considered and complied with in the federal licensure of the Bay region's first nuclear power plant at Calvert Cliffs in Southern Maryland. Later I would spend sixteen years in the Maryland state legislature (1979–1995), where I fought to enact meaningful environmental laws. Nearly every environmental victory with which I have been involved required building underfunded and often fractious environmental coalitions to fight against entrenched and many times well-funded vested interests.

Notable victories during my years in the Maryland Legislature include the Maryland Stormwater Management Act (1982), the Maryland Agricultural Cost Share Program (1982), Maryland Recycling Act (1988), Phosphate Ban (1984), Chesapeake Bay and Endangered Species Income Tax Check-off (1988), Non-Tidal Wetlands Act (1989), and the Forest Conservation Act (1991). Also notable are defeats, including my most regrettable failure, my repeated attempts to require mandatory controls on agricultural pollution, the largest single factor causing the Bay's decline. This legislative push (1989 to 1994) could not overcome the opposition from the farm community, the agricultural lobby and their supporters in the government, and from the Schaefer administration. These mandatory controls are still lacking and are pivotal to Bay restoration.

The Problem with Cleaning Detergents

As discussed in chapter 1, phosphorus and nitrogen are the key pollutants causing the Bay's dead zones and the overall decline of the Bay. In the mid-1980s, one-third of the phosphorus pollution reaching the Bay came from wastewater treatment plants, and 30 percent of this phosphorus came from cleaning detergents. Phosphates serve as builders in detergents, helping in the cleaning and sanitizing process. By 1983, more than two million tons of phosphorus was used annually in US cleaning detergents. Sewage treatment removed only a small percentage of phosphorus from the detergents, creating substantial water quality problems for the country and the Chesapeake Bay.

The first states to react to the problem were Indiana, Michigan, Minnesota, New York, Vermont, and Wisconsin. These states banned phosphates from detergents by 1980, as did Chicago (IL), Akron (OH), and Dade County (FL). In 1977, the Environmental Protection Agency regional administrator urged the adoption of phosphate detergent bans by all Great Lakes Basin jurisdictions. In 1970, Canada enacted its Water Act, which called for an immediate reduction to phosphorus levels in laundry detergents. By the early 1980s, the fight to remove phosphate detergents was on at the national level, and in 1983, I became convinced it was necessary in the Bay states.

Early Efforts to Ban Phosphate Detergents in the Bay States
(1981–1983)

The first attempt to ban phosphates in laundry detergents in Maryland came in the 1981 legislative session when delegate Robin Ficker, a gadfly legislator, introduced HB 167. The vote in the Environmental Matters Committee was 18–1 against the bill, and I was the sole vote in favor. With eleven witnesses signed up against the bill and only three proponents, the bill died a quick and quiet legislative death. With the environmental community distracted by other matters and industry opposed to the ban, this was obviously not going to be an easy sell to the legislature.

In 1983, the six-year, $27 million Environmental Protection Agency Study reaffirmed that nitrogen and phosphorus were the major culprits in the Bay's disastrous decline. High phosphorus loadings were found to seriously affect the freshwater portions of the Bay system. Armed with the new report and having made Bay restoration a campaign issue in 1982, Governor Hughes decided to make 1984 the "Year of the Bay." Governor Hughes assigned key cabinet officers to a group that became known as the Wye Group. They were tasked with developing a comprehensive set of Bay initiatives for the 1984 legislative session. The governor's initiatives included many major legislative proposals, including a controversial restriction of development along the shoreline, but it did not include the phosphate detergent ban. The governor's advisors had considered and rejected the phosphate detergent ban.

While the governor's Wye Group met to focus on Maryland initiatives, a parallel effort was mounted through a set of multistate committees to tackle the broader regional efforts to save the Bay. These multistate working groups were the initial foundation of a conference that would lead to the establishment of the Bay Program. I served on the Land Activities Committee, which was put together for the purpose of making policy recommendations to the Bay governors who would attend what was billed as a landmark conference scheduled for December of 1983. I knew that if I could get the phosphate detergent ban included in the recommendations at the conference, not only would the Wye Group consider supporting a phosphate ban, but there was a chance the other Bay states would get on board.

I made a motion before the Land Activities Committee to recommend the adoption of phosphate bans as part of the Bay restoration efforts. After debate, the motion carried on a 7–6 vote, with the chairman casting the deciding vote and the Chesapeake Bay Foundation representative voting against the measure. I was rather surprised by the Chesapeake Bay Foundation's vote. At this pivotal juncture, the representative from the region's leading environmental group voted against the measure, even after they had testified in favor of Ficker's 1981 phosphate ban. In hindsight, it is now clear that the opposition to the phosphate ban by the Hughes administration and by the Chesapeake Bay Foundation was made for tactical reasons. They were concerned that the ban would be a distraction and jeopardize passage of the Wye Group's Bay initiatives and decided that it would be better to concentrate on upgrading wastewater treatment plants to remove phosphorus, rather than support the controversial ban. I disagreed and believed a phosphate ban would lead to an immediate and tangible reduction in pollution to the Bay, while at the same time saving millions of dollars.

In the end, the key officials who attended the conference in Virginia chose not to approve any specific policy suggestions. Instead they signed a short general statement of support for restoring the Bay and established the Chesapeake Bay Executive Council. This one-half-page statement, which became known as the First Bay Agreement, set the stage for the current voluntary Bay Program. Our committee's recommendation for adoption of phosphate bans was forwarded to the Bay State governors, the mayor of Washington, DC, and the administrator of the EPA, though no jurisdiction included a phosphate ban in their legislative packages. It became clear that specific legislative and regulatory proposals would not be included under the Bay Agreement, and if the phosphate ban was going to pass, it was going to have to be battled out on a state-by-state basis. In Maryland that meant it would be very difficult without the support of the governor and the leading environmental group.

The Struggle Continues (1984)
Unsuccessful in gaining inclusion of a phosphate ban in the Bay initiatives package, on February 3, 1984, I introduced SB 569 in the Maryland Senate to ban phosphates in cleaning agents. Along with me were five Senate cosponsors. The legislation was modeled after similar laws that were enacted in the six states with phosphate bans. It would prohibit the use of phosphates in cleaning agents, including laundry detergents, except for 0.5 percent allowed as incidental to manufacturing. The phosphate ban allowed certain exceptions and permitted a maximum of 8.7 percent phosphorus in automatic dishwashing detergent, as phosphate-free products for automatic dishwasher use were not yet perfected.

Based on the experiences of other states and municipalities, I was convinced that the phosphate ban could quickly and effectively reduce phosphorus flows to the Bay while saving money in wastewater treatment costs. A 1980 EPA study predicted that a Bay-wide phosphate ban would reduce total phosphorus flows to the Bay by 11 percent while reducing the cost of operation and maintenance at sewage treatment plants. It was the right thing to do.

With the legislation introduced, the political lines were drawn. The lobbying against the phosphate ban was furious, as Maryland lobbyists stumbled over themselves to gain national clients such as the Soap and Detergent Association. Conservation groups were joined by the Washington Suburban Sanitary Commission in supporting the bill. The Chesapeake Bay Foundation also supported the effort. The Hughes administration, however, was a different story. Bill Eichbaum, director of Maryland's Office of Environmental Programs, testified at the hearing before the Senate Finance Committee that the phosphate ban would have a very small impact on improving water quality and would have a fiscal impact on his state agency. He recommended a summer study of the bill, which in legislative terms is a way of killing a proposal with kindness.

The finance committee staff report noted that "[t]estimony on the issue was heated and complex with both sides challenging statistics and assumptions of the other side." In addition to the opposition from the director of the State Office of Environmental Programs, opponents who testified among the thirty witnesses included the Maryland Chamber of Commerce; Giant Food; Mid-Atlantic Food Dealers Association; DC, MD, and VA Coin Laundry Association; FMC Corporation; University of Maryland Cooperative Extension Service; and the Soap and Detergent Association.

A witness from the EPA's newly created Chesapeake Bay Program testified, noting that the ban could reduce phosphorus discharges at plants that were not currently removing phosphorus from wastewater by 30 percent. For plants that were currently removing phosphorus, their operating costs could be reduced by 15 percent. He also stated that phosphorus could be reduced at sewage plants without removing phosphorus from detergents. The representative noted that should the legislation pass, consumers would experience increased cleaning costs for hot water, bleach, and fabric softener of $7.70 per household per year, and that there were other strategies to be used to reduce phosphorus. When specifically asked if he supported the ban, the EPA spokesman told the committee that the EPA had no position on the phosphate ban, and it was strictly a state and local decision. It seemed odd that the Bay Program had no position on such a policy proposal and certainly did not help the cause.

Despite the successful implementation of phosphate bans in the other states and despite the development of effective phosphate-free detergents, on February 28, 1984, the committee voted to defeat the bill on a 6–2 vote and appoint a subcommittee to study the legislation. The blistering lobbying barrage, opposition by the Hughes administration, and the failure of the Bay Program to aggressively support the measure had killed the bill.

In May 1984, a four-member Subcommittee on Phosphates was appointed by the Senate Finance Committee. The subcommittee recommended that consideration of a phosphate ban be deferred until there was a more concerted effort to adopt such bans in other Bay states. The subcommittee cited a pending Virginia study on a phosphate ban. On January 6, 1985, the Subcommittee on Phosphates issued a new finding that the "[s]ubcommittee makes no recommendation concerning" a phosphate ban, although they noted that excessive phosphate enrichment should be dealt with as expeditiously as possible. The Hughes administration had testified before the subcommittee in the fall still in opposition to the phosphate ban.

The subcommittee's recommendations were passed on to the Senate Economic and Environmental Affairs Committee, which was expanded from the Economic Affairs Committee and now had jurisdiction over all such environmental issues as part of a major Senate reorganization completed in October 1984. In addition, a new chairman was assigned for the merged Senate Economic and Environmental Affairs Committee who was supportive of the phosphate ban, replacing senator Jerome Connell, who opposed the ban. These were all fortuitous developments enhancing chances of passage of a phosphate ban.

Success (1985)

On January 17, 1985, along with seven cosponsors, I introduced a new phosphate ban bill, SB 277. I distinctly recall recruiting Senate cosponsors and approaching senator Leo Green, a previous cosponsor and solid conservation vote. He had chaired the Subcommittee on Phosphates and at first balked at cosponsoring the new bill, advising me that the bill needed to be changed and it couldn't pass without change. Finally I said, "Leo, the bill models the other state phosphate bans, and we cannot change much." Senator Green did decide to cosponsor and fully supported the measure.

With passage of the 1984 Bay Initiatives completed, the environmental community rallied in support of the phosphate ban, and efforts began to overcome an army of industry lobbyists. More than $650,000 was paid to seventeen lobbyists to fight the legislation. This was in addition to in-house lobbyists employed by some organizations.

I later realized that I had inadvertently helped some lobbyists raise enough money to pay for their children's college education.

Adding to the importance of the Maryland phosphate ban was the recognition of the leadership role that Maryland was playing in the Bay restoration—if Maryland defeated the measure, the other Bay states would probably do so as well, a fact that was well known to industry leaders.

The face-off began at a hearing of the newly configured Senate Economic and Environmental Affairs Committee on February 14, where the Hughes administration reversed its previous opposition and supported the phosphate ban. All of Maryland's conservation groups and the national Environmental Policy Institute joined in supporting SB 277. Also in support were the Chesapeake Bay Commission, Maryland Waterman's Association, League of Women Voters, Washington Suburban Sanitary Commission, Baltimore County, and the Maryland Conference of Local Environmental Health Directors. The supporters detailed why the phosphate ban should be enacted:

1. Quick reductions of 11 to 13 percent of phosphorus loadings to the Bay.
2. Only a small percent of Maryland's sewage treatment plants were equipped to remove phosphorus.
3. Maryland wastewater treatment plants would save more than $4 million per year in operating cost.
4. Maryland wastewater treatment plants would reduce their sludge disposal needs.
5. Passage would prod other Bay states to take similar actions.
6. Studies from the Great Lakes states with phosphate bans indicated virtually no problems with consumers.

Lined up in opposition were the Maryland Chamber of Commerce; Baltimore City (mayor William Donald Schaefer presiding); Giant Food; Mid-Atlantic Food Dealers Association; DC, MD, and VA Coin Laundry Association; Procter and Gamble; FMC Corporation; University of Maryland Cooperative Extension Service; the Soap and Detergent Association; the Chemical Specialties Manufacturers Association; and several hired university Ph.D.s. Opponents' arguments against the phosphate ban included:

1. The ban would have very little, if any, water quality benefits, and efforts should be concentrated on phosphorus removal at wastewater treatment plants.
2. Consumers would wind up paying a lot more because of the increased

costs associated with using more detergent, more additives and softeners, more hot water, more washing machine repairs, and more damage
to clothing.

3. The ban would have a devastating impact on Laundromat operators,
   ruining their washing machines, causing repair bills to sky rocket, and
   requiring the use of more hot water.
4. Personal hygiene would be affected, particularly with undergarments.
5. Baltimore City argued that the phosphate ban could potentially affect
   more than 1,000 industry jobs in the Baltimore area.

On February 28, the Senate Economic and Environmental Affairs Committee adopted minor amendments to the bill, including the addition of
another cosponsor, and passed the bill on to the full Senate on a 7–4 vote.
Despite delays on the Senate floor and attempts to defeat the legislation, the
full Senate passed SB 277 on a vote of 39–5. Lobbying pressure had already
shifted to the House, where passage was still problematic. Delegate James
McClellan (an opponent of the ban and a member of the Chesapeake Bay
Commission that was designed to promote pro-Bay policies) taunted me
about the legislation, saying, "It may have passed the Senate, but let's see you
get it out of the House." He was also a member of the Environmental Matters
Committee with jurisdiction over the legislation. His opposition was going
to be a problem.

As the focus shifted from the Senate to the House, the lobbying effort
against SB 277 became extremely intense. The *Baltimore Sun* quoted delegate Larry LaMotte of the Environmental Matters Committee, "You can't go
to the bathroom without having somebody right behind you waiting to talk.
There are more lobbyists per square delegate than on any issue in recent
memory." Delegate Bill McCaffrey, the vice chairman of the committee who
very deftly handled SB 277 on the House floor, said, "In eleven years I
haven't seen anything lobbied like this."

The army of lobbyists and their unseemly tactics began to backfire, as the
popular press seized on the issue. Articles appeared in the press about a seem-
ingly fraudulent effort to pay workers up to $1 per signature ($50 bonus for
first 100 signatures) on a petition against the ban. A public relations firm was
paid to cook up the idea for this group dubbed CLEAN, for Consumers
League for Environmental Action Now. They used Chesapeake Bay Foundation's recognizable blue and white Save the Bay colors and declared: CLEAN
THE BAY. BUT DO IT RIGHT. CLEAN alleged that the ban would do
little to help water quality, but do a lot to harm consumers. Unaware citizens

were recruited and trained, thinking they were working to help clean the Bay.

The ruse was exposed when one housewife soliciting signatures at a food store was told by a member of the environmental community that the ban was a sound way to help restore the Bay and had the support of the conservation community. The startled petitioner then agreed to appear at a press conference arranged by the Chesapeake Bay Foundation to expose this industry attempt to defeat the ban. More than 1,800 signatures had been collected by March 7 when the scam was exposed. The outrage over this well-funded effort helped build momentum for the ban. At the House hearing on March 27 on SB 277, when legislators asked who was responsible for funding and running CLEAN, not one of the many opponents in the hearing room would take credit, angering some legislators.

The credibility of the opposition continued to erode. Research revealed that a box of Procter and Gamble's powdered Tide detergent sold in New York (a phosphate-ban state) did not call for any additional additives, water softeners, hot water, or different washing conditions than the Tide sold in Maryland. The boxes were identical except for the phosphate content.

Baltimore mayor William Donald Schaefer stepped up opposition to the phosphate ban. Baltimore was home to a Procter and Gamble plant, as well as Lever Brothers and FMC, all companies that would supposedly be affected by the law. It appeared that these industries had lobbied Mayor Schaefer successfully against the phosphate ban despite data that showed that Baltimore wastewater plants would save more than $500,000 annually in treatment costs. The union at Procter and Gamble's Baltimore plant also chimed in against SB 277, which could have been a serious blow to the proposal. Schaefer's lobbyist wrote legislators that the phosphate ban put more than 1,000 jobs at stake. Since there was a large Baltimore City legislative delegation and because of the sensitivity to job losses in manufacturing, this claim of large job losses could have doomed passage.

With the entire environmental community now supporting the ban, we were able to debunk the job-loss claim. Officials at the Chesapeake Bay Foundation contacted leaders at the supposedly affected industries. Through their discussions they were able to document that there would be little or no job impact from a phosphate ban at the Maryland plants, a fact that was reported by the press.

The grassroots campaign in favor of the legislation was led by people like John Kabler of Clean Water Action and Chuck Fox of the Environmental Policy Institute and many other groups, including the Chesapeake Bay Foundation. Perhaps the most effective tactic of the environmental community was to use the aggressive methods of the industry lobbyists to undermine the industry position. Given the media attention, the legislature and the governor were under a great deal of pressure not to succumb to these moneyed-interests and their army of well-paid lobbyists. The environmental community effectively framed the issue as a campaign against the well-heeled special interests and their supporters in government.

The support of the Washington Suburban Sanitary Commission also helped the legislation, as the commission exerted influence on the large delegations representing Prince George's and Montgomery counties ringing Washington, DC. Even House opponents of the phosphate ban felt compelled to pass a bill, if for no other reason than to show that they "stood up" to the industry lobbyists. On March 29, with 10 days left in the legislative session, the Environmental Matters Committee significantly amended SB 277 and passed a gutted version of the bill on to the House floor.

The bill had been greatly compromised with amendments designed to cripple it. One amendment exempted all households with septic systems. Another exempted all coin-operated Laundromats. Another exempted all federal government facilities. These amendments would make the ban impossible to implement, and their authors knew it.

On April 3, the House of Delegates voted in favor of the weakened bill (79–48) and passed the bill to the Senate. The president of the Senate then asked me if I could live with the amendments, as not accepting them with just four days left in the session would jeopardize passage. I advised him that the Senate should reject the amendments and I asked him to appoint three conferees that would stand tall in negotiations with the House conferees. Such a six-person conference committee is routinely appointed to work out differences between the houses on legislation. I realized that not accepting the House amendments might doom the legislation, as there was little time left until the session would end, and any delays by either house could kill the bill. On April 4, the president did appoint three strong Senate conferees who were phosphate ban supporters. The House did not appoint their conferees until April 6.

The lobbying and media pressure had reached a crescendo. On April 2, the *Washington Post* editorialized in support of the ban "Who Will Vote Against the Bay?" stating, "Those lawmakers who are serious about saving the bay should recognize and resist the tactics of the detergent lobby—namely, to weaken the house version of the bill enough to provide an excuse to kill it . . . Despite the failure so far of house leaders to rally votes for the phosphate ban, individual delegates should see the importance of supporting a bill that would serve as a start on even more effective moves to save the bay."

On April 3, the *Baltimore Sun* editorialized "Amending the Ban to Death," accusing the House Environmental Matters Committee of using "an old back-door tactic to reduce any chance of passing the bill" by skillfully weakening it by adding exemptions that would gut the bill. The *Sun* urged prompt passage by the House so a conference committee could put the bill back to its original version before the session ended in a week.

The conferees met and deleted the offending exemptions: the septic system exemption, the coin-operated Laundromat exemption, and the federal government exemption. A sunset provision was adopted that would terminate the law in four years if further legislative action was not taken. In the end, Maryland delegate James McClellan was the only conference committee member who refused to sign off on the compromise. The conference committee report was not completed and signed until the last day of session, April 8. The measure was quickly rushed to the desks of both houses that evening, where the Senate passed SB 277 on a 37–8 vote and the House by an 85–47 vote. Governor Hughes signed the bill in May 1985, and it went into effect on December 1, 1985.

Epilogue
Flush with this success, I testified before the Washington, DC, city council on their phosphate ban legislation, and the district implemented a ban in September 1986. Virginia implemented a phosphate ban in January 1988. Pennsylvania implemented a ban in March 1990. And in 1988, I introduced legislation into the Maryland legislature, along with 27 Senate cosponsors, to remove the four-year sunset provision. By this time the controversy was over; Governor Schaefer, who had strongly opposed the initial bill while mayor of Baltimore, and delegate James McClellan, who had opposed the bill throughout the process, voted to repeal the sunset.

On June 25, 1987, the state environmental agency made its first report on the effectiveness of the Maryland phosphate ban. The report documented the ban's success—a 16 to 21 percent reduction in phosphorous loads to the Bay and annual saving of about $4 million, as well as total consumer acceptance. Other states realized similar phosphorus reductions and cost savings. These savings continue today.

Even industry leaders seemed to have warmed up to the ban. Giant Food, a major Maryland employer, had vigorously opposed the phosphate ban in

1984 and 1985, but supported the sunset repeal. After Washington, DC, adopted the phosphate ban, Giant Food reversed positions and took out full-page newspaper ads in support of the ban in Virginia, touting Giant's support for cleaning up the Bay. The reality was that Giant's major product distribution system would be much simpler with the same phosphate-free detergents for the region. By 1994, due to the actions by state legislatures forcing the detergent industry to remove phosphates and two decades of development of effective phosphate-free detergents, the industry no longer used phosphates in laundry detergents in the United States.

While we won the phosphate battle, there are plenty more battles to be fought in the ongoing war to save the Bay. It is absolutely essential to enact major land use legislation that forces compact development and to establish a no-net-loss of forest policy. It is essential to establish a policy of no-net-increase in water pollution flows from new development and to systematically retrofit existing urban storm-water flows. Equally important is the need to adopt legislation to require enforceable best management practices on all farmland and to give forest conservation on farmland the highest priority in state agricultural land preservation efforts. Of course, many arguments have been and will be raised against such changes, as they were against the phosphate ban, but unless our leaders have the political courage to tackle these important issues and take on entrenched special interests, the Bay is doomed.

The Long Fight

Guest entry by Tyla Matteson (with Glen Besa)

Getting Involved
The first I heard about the idea to build a massive reservoir in King William County, Virginia, was on June 18, 1991, more than eighteen years ago. My mother and I were on a field trip in the county learning more about tree harvesting by the Chesapeake Corporation. As we picnicked on the banks of the Mattaponi River, one of the luncheon speakers who addressed our group was a slight man who spoke with great urgency.

This man was Webster (Little Eagle) Custalow, chief of the Mattaponi tribe, and he emphatically stated that the proposed reservoir should not be built. He explained that the project would have an earthen dam that could fail and endanger lives. But more generally, he argued that the reservoir would be wrong for the river. "We must," he said, "think back seven generations and look ahead seven generations" before making important decisions.

His words made a lasting impression on me. In a very real way, Chief Custalow's plea gave birth to the "save the Mattaponi" effort that would last more than a decade and would eventually include the work of countless dedicated volunteers.[2]

Some time later, a news article announced a public hearing for the reservoir to be held in rural King William County, site of the proposed reservoir. Remembering chief Webster Custalow's impassioned words, I drove seventy miles to attend the presentation. The hearing was led by Newport News Waterworks staff, and their objective was to gain public support for the plan to build what was originally designed to be a massive 2,200-acre reservoir. The reservoir would be filled by diverting millions of gallons of water per day from the Mattaponi River to fill Cohoke Creek Valley, on Cohoke Creek, a tributary of the Pamunkey River. The City of Newport News formed a coalition called the Regional Raw Water Study Group, which included the localities of Hampton, Poquoson, York County, James City County, and Newport News. Newport News stated that the King William Reservoir would be a regional solution to meet the future water needs of the Virginia Peninsula.

At the hearing, held at Acquinton Elementary School, the public was divided into three groups and moved from one room to another, where the pro-reservoir officials made their case. By good fortune, a local resident who shared my concern over the project, William Perritt, was in my group. William asked many questions, including detailed questions about how salinity changes caused by the massive water withdrawals might harm the river. While the waterworks staff provided answers, none of their assurances could satisfy our concerns. After the hearing, standing in front of the elementary school, three of us, William Perritt, Shirley (Little Dove) Custalow McGowan (the daughter of Chief Custalow), and I discussed the evening's events. We were very concerned.

Shortly after the hearing, William Perritt accepted an invitation from the York River Group of the Sierra Club to drive to the Virginia Peninsula to bring us up to speed. After listening to William's concerns, our group immediately decided to become more deeply involved in the issue. I visited Chief Custalow at his home on the small Mattaponi Indian Tribe reservation, on the banks of the Mattaponi River, and he asked the Sierra Club to help. In 1996 the York River Group formalized its opposition to the reservoir, based on the harm to the environment and the harm to the Mattaponi tribe. Our work broadened when the entire Virginia Chapter of the Sierra Club embraced the campaign to stop the reservoir. Chief Custalow was no longer speaking alone.

We quickly began to organize our political effort to stop the reservoir. Bob Bingaman, Sierra Club national field director, was invited to a Virginia Chapter meeting in 1996, and he walked us through the process of engaging in a full-fledged environmental campaign. He passed out a handbook called *Enough Is Enough: The Hellraiser's Guide to Community Activism*. We also studied the Sierra Club's *Grassroots Organizing Training Manual*. We believed we could do this, but for many of us this was our introduction to developing an environmental campaign plan, and we had no idea how the process would ultimately work.

That same summer we formed the Alliance to Save the Mattaponi, in the backyard of Joanne Fridley's family home. On the banks of the Mattaponi River, with about a dozen local people, many of whom are still in the fight today, we pledged our support to save the Mattaponi and to block the reservoir. At the meeting, we rejected the general impression that the King William Reservoir was a done deal. We were not sure how we could possibly block a project that had the full support of the state's political and economic establishment, but we knew we were going to try.

Some of our initial steps included identifying our allies and our opponents. One of our greatest political allies was state delegate Jo Ann Davis, who in 2001 was elected US congresswoman from the First District of Virginia, where the reservoir was to be built. She helped until she passed away in 2007, two years prior to our latest victory. Other elected officials who helped our cause and who testified for the Mattaponi were state delegates Albert Pollard, Harvey Morgan, and Ryan McDougle (now a state senator).

Most of the Peninsula mayors were pro-reservoir. Other pro-reservoir entities included the chamber of commerce, the Peninsula Home Builders, a significant portion of the business community, the editorial board of the principal Peninsula newspaper (*The Daily Press*), governor Jim Gilmore, and US senator John Warner. On the Newport News City Council, only one member, Madeline McMillan, was against the project, and she stayed steadfast and vocal, despite great pressure.

Though the pro-reservoir side was politically well connected, we truly believed that justice favored our side. The compelling story of the Mattaponi Indian Tribe's opposition to the reservoir prompted thousands of people to get actively involved in the permitting process, and helped turn public opinion in our direction. The issue was not simply another "not in my back yard" (NIMBY) environmental cause, it was also about defending a native culture that has relied on the Mattaponi River for generations. In June of 1996, the Mattaponi tribe held a pow-wow, and we were there with a Save the Mattaponi booth. While our interests were in line, we were always careful never to speak for the tribe. We were building trust and lasting friendships that would support us through the long campaign; we were truly united in opposition to the reservoir.

The first director of Virginia's Sierra Club chapter, Albert Pollard, took a strong interest in the campaign and was instrumental in moving the alliance forward. He continues to help with the project, now serving as Virginia state delegate from the Northern Neck. Many thousands of people have helped in one way or another, from signing postcards destined for various decision makers, to attending and speaking at the many state and federal hearings. If we were going to defeat the project, we were going to do it based on the strength of our argument and the dedication of our supporters.

One fine lady who I spoke to two to three times a week in the early years was Margaret Linton. With her amazing drive and persistence, she contacted every environmental organization and every individual she could identify for their support. Margaret made posters for the first pow-wow and the first Walkerton Day tabling event. When she died in 2001, her two daughters, Larkin and Temple, held a commemoration of her life at her river home in Aylett. With the assistance of long-time Alliance friend Tom Rubino, in his small boat, her ashes were spread in the river she loved and worked so hard to protect. Another strong supporter who passed away before the conclusion of the campaign was William Todd Henley. Upon his death, he asked that donations be made to the Alliance to Save the Mattaponi. This is how we were going to win the fight, from the energy that comes from people fighting for something they truly love.

We found people willing to help by signing petitions and postcards by the thousands. We set up tables or booths several times a year, at the Richmond Easter Parade, Cary Street Watermelon Festival, and in the annual Walkerton Day parade and the West Point Crab Carnival. We have given away scores of "Save the Mattaponi" bumper stickers and yard signs. The sentiment has always been, and continues to be, favorable for protecting the Mattaponi River and respecting the Mattaponi Indian Tribe's treaty rights to the river.

Our best allies are about a dozen Alliance members who have been fighting the reservoir since we began the campaign in 1996. They are all volunteers and are willing to help at the events, year after year. It is a kind of labor of love. Over the years we have met at people's homes, and sometimes at the Babyak's camp meeting room, on the Mattaponi River. We have received help from many groups and individuals, such as the Mattaponi and Pamunkey River Association and the Ruritans, and several artists have contributed to the cause. There have been no environmental groups in favor of the reservoir.

Financial contributions from supporters have allowed us to print flyers, cover costs associated with legal work (provided pro bono by the Southern Environmental Law Center), and to pay for consultants' reports. The Chesapeake Bay Foundation and the Sierra Club were significant partners with the Alliance. The campaign is a genuine wish for justice, for the river, and for those who depend on the river.

What Was at Stake?

People like Margaret Linton and William Todd Henley understood that the river was a treasure to cherish. If Newport News were to build this reservoir, it would draw up to 75 million gallons of water per day from the Mattaponi, changing the salinity of the river and impeding the recovery process of the depleted shad fishery. While the City of Newport News proposed a moratorium on withdrawals during spawning season, when juvenile shad would be imperiled by the project's pipes, nothing would prevent withdrawals in cases of drought or other emergencies. Moreover, over 400 acres of wetlands would be destroyed by the large 1,500-acre lake, the single greatest loss of wetlands since the passage of the Clean Water Act of 1972. Two identified endangered species, the sensitive joint vetch of the pea family and the small whorled pogonia of the orchid family, would also be harmed by the project.

The Native Americans of the region would lose about 100 archaeological sites of importance, which would be inundated by the reservoir. Their historic ties to the Mattaponi River and their dependence on the river for sustenance were also at risk by the project. A treaty signed in 1677 specifically stated that no edifice could be constructed within three miles of the reservation. For the Mattaponi and Pamunkey, the only two reservated Virginia tribes, the proposed reservoir was yet another broken promise in a long list of abuses suffered by native people. To this day, the tribes honor the treaty every year, at Thanksgiving, with a gift to the governor of Virginia.

The Alliance and the Virginia tribes have participated in numerous events over the years in opposition to the reservoir, but one of the best-remembered events was the Trail of Hope symbolic walk on May 15, 1999. The walk began in Jamestown and drew more than 600 participants, forming a long line behind the tribal members, who carried large banners saying Save the Mattaponi. After the walk, several participants made speeches in opposition to the reservoir. Assistant Mattaponi chief Carl Custalow said these memorable words: "If we destroy our natural resources, everyone pays." Dr. Thomasina Jordan, well known for her work for the American Indians of Virginia, showed great courage delivering her speech. She was ill from a devastating bout with cancer and passed away eight days later.

The First Test

We knew that if we could block the State Water Control Board permit or the US Army Corps of Engineer permit, two essential steps in the reservoir project, we could slow or maybe even defeat the reservoir, so this is where we spent our initial effort. Every permit was another opportunity to save the Mattaponi, and we made the most of each one. Agency staff later told us that they had never seen so many petitions and letters in opposition to a project, nor had they seen so many individuals passionately participate at the public hearings. We hired consultants to help us develop formal comments to the US Army Corps of Engineers and the State Water Control Board, and we raised funds in order to pay for their services; other consultants donated their time.

Though we packed the room on December 16, 1997, at the State Water Control Board meeting, we were outmaneuvered by the pro-reservoir side. Officials from the City of Newport News arranged for two busloads of pro-reservoir supporters to attend the meeting. The board chairman stated that his heart said one thing but his head said another. The chairman and all the board members but one voted to grant the water permit. The vote was a big blow to our side. We now knew that if we were going to compete in this fight, we were going to have to step up our efforts.

We then sent thousands of comments to the Corps of Engineers. Colonel Allan Carroll of the Norfolk District and his staff gathered thousands of pages of testimony. In 2001, in a document over 300 pages long, Colonel Carroll shocked the political establishment of the state when he sided with us and denied a key permit to Newport News. He based his decision on the harm to the environment, to the American Indians, and on the lack of documented need for water. Both sides had submitted water need studies; our side found that Newport News had significantly overstated their water need projections, and independent studies by the Corps agreed with our experts' projections.

Despite our success, we would later learn that some bad ideas do not die easily in the Commonwealth, especially those backed by the state's governor. In an unprecedented move, governor Jim Gilmore challenged the Norfolk District's decision, which elevated the decision to the North Atlantic Division of the Corps of Engineers. We then sent letters to general Stephen Rhoades, for a total of some 4,000 comments, asking that he deny the permit for the reservoir. Also, recommendations from the US Environmental Protection Agency and the US Fish and Wildlife Service were submitted requesting a denial, based on environmental harm and availability of drinking water from alternative sources.

On August 5, 2001, thirteen of us, including the three adult children of Chief Custalow, piled into a rented bus from Richmond to hold a rally in a small city park near the Corps offices in New York City. The objective was to somehow influence General Rhoades, who would make the ultimate decision on the federal permit. Shirley (Little Dove) Custalow, Edith (White Feather) Custalow, and Linwood (Little Bear) Custalow performed special Native American dances, and then invited the participants to join in the Round Dance, forming a circle to represent unity. This incredible journey helped bond our friendships and cement our commitment.

Weighing in to support the reservoir were senator John Warner, Newport News mayor Joe Frank, and probusiness individuals from the Virginia Peninsula area. In September of 2002, and with little explanation for their determination, the North Atlantic Division of the Corps of Engineers, under General Rhoades' direction, overrode the Norfolk District and issued a permit for the reservoir. With allies at the Southern Environmental Law Center, the Sierra Club, and the Chesapeake Bay Foundation, the Alliance to Save the Mattaponi decided to appeal the decision in federal court. Although we had lost the first round, we were determined to keep on fighting.

Round Two (2003)

Newport News also needed to obtain a permit from the Virginia Marine Resources Commission (VMRC) in order to build an intake structure on the Mattaponi River. The stated mission of the VMRC is to provide stewardship of Virginia's marine and aquatic resources and tidal waters, present and future, and we were fortunate to have board members on the commission who took this mission seriously. Board members are appointed by the governor for four-year staggered terms, which meant not all of them were Gilmore appointees. Moreover, scientists from the state's premier environmental science center, the Virginia Institute of Marine Science, recommended against the reservoir because of the potential impact to the shad fishery.

On April 22, 2003, a record number of people attended a hearing of the VMRC at Warwick High School in Newport News. By midnight, only a few citizens had spoken, since the hearing was dominated by an initial presentation from Newport News, followed by a long lineup of area mayors, all of whom spoke in favor of the project. A decision was made to continue the hearing, and a follow-up meeting was scheduled for May 14, 2003, at the VMRC hearing room in downtown Newport News. Another record number attended, and we were given the chance to voice our position. The project was still wrong, for all the reasons we had stated before. When the vote was taken, our side won by a vote of 6–2. The permit for a water intake structure was denied.

Though we had won for a second time, officials at Newport News immediately challenged the decision. They filed a legal appeal and also pursued the issue in the Virginia General Assembly session of 2004, with several bills introduced that threatened the authority of the agency. Political pressure, combined with a legal settlement, prompted the VMRC to reopen the process, and another hearing on the permit was scheduled in Williamsburg on August 11 and 12, 2004. When the commission voted on the issue for a second time, they did so with three new members, all of whom voted to grant the permit. We lost the 2004 vote by a margin of 5–3. Newport News got their permit, although there were a number of limits on withdrawals during the shad spawning season. The bottom line was that we had lost.

The VMRC decision was crushing. I watched as our colleagues who had witnessed the hearing walked out of the high school, some in tears. We all have our heroic moments; one of mine occurred that evening in the rear of the auditorium, as I pulled a stack of petitions from my bag that requested a Coastal Zone Management hearing. I asked a few people to sign on their way out. In other words, the fight was not over.

Round Three
Throughout the campaign, we had won several fights, first with the Corps of Engineers Norfolk District, but the victory was taken away when Governor Gilmore objected and elevated the decision to the North Atlantic District. Then we won with the VMRC, in a stunning 6–2 vote, only to have Newport News pressure the commission to reverse their decision and issue the permit. In 2007, the State Water Control Board denied an extension to their 1997 permit in another packed hearing, but reversed their decision at their next meeting. Once again we had "won," only to lose in a subsequent administrative hearing.

It seems that our opponents were not willing to take no for an answer, nor were they willing to play by the rules. We have a list of objectionable tactics

TIMELINE

1984: The Norfolk District of the Corps of Engineers publishes a water supply study that projects that the Lower Peninsula of Virginia will need 40 million gallons a day of additional water by 2030.

1987: Newport News organizes the Regional Raw Water Study Group to develop a plan to meet future water needs.

1993: Newport News, on behalf of the study group, seeks permits from the Corps and the Virginia Department of Environmental Quality for a reservoir on Cahoke Creek, a tributary of the Pamunkey River. The reservoir would be filled with water pumped from the Mattaponi River.

1994: The Corps issues a draft environmental impact study for the project, which is revised in 1995, with a final study issued in 1997.

1999: The Corps' Institute for Water Resources re-examines the future water projections and concludes that the water shortfall would be closer to 24 million gallons a day by 2040.

2001: The Corps' Norfolk District recommends against issuing a wetlands permit, saying "it is not reasonable to build such an environmentally damaging project to satisfy a need that may never materialize." Then-governor Jim Gilmore appeals the decision to the Corps' North Atlantic Division.

2002: The Corps' North Atlantic Division determines that the reservoir is the "least damaging practicable alternative" to meet the region's long-term water needs.

2003: The Virginia Marine Resources Commission denies a permit for the water intake on the Mattaponi River based on studies indicating it was in the midst of the state's most productive shad spawning area.

2004: Under heavy political pressure, the VMRC reverses its decision and approves the permit with restrictions on when water could be withdrawn from the Mattaponi River.

2005: The Corps issues a wetlands permit for the reservoir. Although the projected shortfall for 2040 was now 15.9 million gallons a day, the Corps says the project is the least damaging practical alternative. The EPA chooses not to veto the permit.

2009: The US District Court for the District of Columbia invalidates the Corps' permit, saying it acted "arbitrarily and capriciously" in approving it.

Source: Karl Blankenship, 2009. "Court Rules Against Permit for Reservoir." The Bay Journal (Vol. 19, No. 3).

used by Newport News over the years. One of these occurred at Hampton Bay Days in September of 2000, when the Sierra Club tabler was told we could not have petitions signed opposing the reservoir. However, at another booth at the same event, an environmental group was allowed to get signatures relating to a different issue. A *Daily Press* reporter brought attention to this injustice with a story about the abrogation of freedom of speech.

On March 31, 2009, we received the heartening news that we have been waiting for since the campaign began thirteen years earlier; a US District Court judge overturned the Corps' permit for the project, ruling that the project was unnecessarily destructive to the environment. In accordance with the ruling, on April 30, 2009, the Norfolk District commander of the Corps of Engineers directed all activities previously authorized by the permit to stop. The U.S. district judge Henry Kennedy Jr. agreed with our claim that drowning 403 acres of wetlands was not the "least damaging practical alternative" to meeting the water needs of the City of Newport News. He went on to say the Corps acted "arbitrarily and capriciously" when approving the project and also criticized the Environmental Protection Agency for not vetoing the permit.

Since 1987, the City of Newport News has spent $50 million on the project, covering environmental engineering, legal, and some land acquisition costs. It is not known what the final outcome will be, but it is hoped that Newport News will finally abandon this unpopular project. Newport News Waterworks provides good drinking water to the several localities they service on the Lower Peninsula. We are confident that Newport News Waterworks can meet the future needs of the region more than adequately without the King William Reservoir. We remain committed to stopping the reservoir and saving the Mattaponi River.

To learn more about our ongoing campaign to save the river, visit our website at www.savethemattaponi.org.

No Safe Way

Guest entry by Mike Shay
Bill Kirchen, formerly of Commander Cody and His Lost Planet Airmen, was tearing the house down with songs like "Too Much Fun" and "Hot Rod Lincoln." The event was conceived as an "almost victory party," a celebration of a six-year environmental battle that was finally over, but a war that never seemed to end. The party gave us a chance to celebrate and cement

the commitments that we had won from key elected officials in our latest fight and to reenergize our volunteers for the work ahead. More than anything else, it was an example of our commitment to have fun while we worked to make a difference.

In our volunteer environmental organization, South Arundel Citizens for Responsible Development (SACReD), it has always been my job to find the talent in our community, glue it together, and to help find creative ways to keep the effort energized. Years in the environmental trenches have taught me that there is nothing more energizing than success and having fun. And we certainly needed renewed energy after our long struggle to protect 550 acres of some of the most beautiful and wild coastline left along the Chesapeake Bay, a piece of land located in rural southern Anne Arundel County that the developers and their allies in government called Baldwin's Choice, but everyone else referred to as Franklin Point.

In the end, we stayed true to our cause and successfully saved this incredible land from development and inappropriate proposals by our local government, but the success did not come without a price. The most trying time during the ordeal, and turning point in the campaign, was surviving a $50 million defamation lawsuit aimed at us by the would-be developer. The lawsuit led to a three-week jury trial in Washington, DC, and thanks to an outstanding pro bono defense provided by one of the largest law firms in the region, we prevailed. Not only did we successfully defend ourselves, in the end, we defended Franklin Point, which was cause enough for celebration.

A longtime state delegate from the district shared her perspective on the fight with a reporter from the *Baltimore Sun*: ". . . SACReD show(ed) that with tenaciousness, they can and will win. They are like bulldogs." Equally revealing was the developer's perspective shared in the same *Baltimore Sun* article. "I just gave up and joined them," he said. "Anyone who works as hard as they do is going to be a problem for someone like me."[3] The accomplishment of saving this important property empowered and emboldened our group. We left the Franklin Point effort believing that if we had patience and creativity, and stayed focused, we might very well save a rural community from sprawl development and maybe, just maybe, the Bay itself might have a chance. But little did we know that our wild ride had just begun.

Having defeated a millionaire developer, we now faced a billon-dollar big box developer—Safeway Corporation. This fight was about even more than preserving an environmental gem; it was about preserving the character and integrity of our rural community. The proposed project would harm our local independent businesses, create incentives for future development in the area, bring traffic to the community, harm our water quality, and forever change the very character of our historic fishing and farming community. Suburbia had arrived at our rural doorstep, and it was an unwelcome guest.

While we were determined to preserve our community, we were not eager for a fight. The attorneys who had defended us in the Franklin Point case counseled us to talk to Safeway Corporation and try to come to a compromise, especially before entering into another full-fledged campaign, advice we were happy to accept.[4] We attended the meeting in good faith and attempted to broaden our coalition by bringing respected business and community leaders from outside of our group. We met Safeway's East Coast leadership at their corporate headquarters in Lanham, Maryland, where they delivered a presentation that they thought would impress us, but in fact confirmed our worst fears.

Safeway planned their largest-sized store for our rural community, and eight additional "pad sites" for national retail chain stores. They rounded out their proposed strip mall with 50,000 square feet of parking to accommodate the shoppers that would have to travel through our community to satisfy Safeway's oversize plan. We asked the Safeway officials to share the economic basis for their business plan, in an attempt to understand how they thought a mall of this size could survive in a town of less than ten thousand people, without becoming destination shopping. They refused to be candid, and more importantly refused to compromise in terms of downsizing the project to meet the real needs of our community. Before the meeting was over, we knew we were in for a fight, but this time our all-volunteer group was going to face a billion-dollar corporation as well as the leadership of our own county government.

To smooth the way for the development, county planners went against the wishes of the community and designated the area a "primary growth area," which led three big box grocery stores to set their sights on us in what was referred to in the newspapers as "Store Wars." We countered by demanding that the Army Corps of Engineers hold a public meeting on the topic. SACReD, along with local politicians, wrote letters to the Corps and, of course, we notified the local media.[5] The basis of our argument was that the Corps should reexamine its existing wetlands permit, as wetlands had grown in the area since their last permit. While the move was a long shot to say the least, the Corps rarely supported our efforts; it was our first opportunity to increase public awareness of the issue and to earn some much-needed media attention. To win this battle we knew it was important to get the media interested in the topic. As was expected, the Corps refused to hold public hearings, which led to this coverage in the *Baltimore Sun*:

> "Well, yes, they are not required to hold a hearing," Spake [SACReD board member] said. "But if a U.S. senator and state delegates ask them to, don't you think they should? I mean, how much political pressure do they need? Does Al Gore have to call them and ask for it?[6]

One month after refusing to hold a public meeting, the Corps automatically renewed the wetlands permit. The Corps' resistance made the issue newsworthy and gave the campaign the attention it desperately needed. The *Baltimore Sun* wrote:

> Michael Shay, one of SACReD's leaders, said yesterday that he spoke several times to Linda Morrison, the Corps' chief of regulation, before the permit expired, but she refused to hold a meeting. Shay said "she had always been cooperative when he had worked with her in SACReD's fight against a housing development a few years ago." This time, however, she kept asking him to call her back, he said . . . "This was the first time she has ever dodged me."[7]

The media strategy was working, as we were able to portray ourselves as the voice of reason and the Corps as pushing through the permit. We were beginning the long process of framing the issue in our favor, and when we would take more aggressive steps in the future, as we would certainly have to, the public would understand the source of our frustration.[8] The first turning point in the campaign happened a month later and is summed up in the opening sentence of a *Baltimore Sun* story titled "Mall Foes Prepare Anew for Battle."[9] The article read:

> Opponents of the long-contested plans for a Safeway strip mall in Deale are posting signs throughout south Anne Arundel County, stuffing fliers into grocery bags and making buttons in preparation for another battle. The Army Corps of Engineers has scheduled a public forum.

We won the battle for the public forum and we were moving public support in our favor, but we knew if we were going to prevail we would have to address our chief political obstacle—county executive Janet Owens. Owens had a well-earned reputation among the area's environmental community for her "Install the Sprawl" approach to local development. Not only could we count on her not to support our cause, we knew from the outset that she was a driving force behind the sprawl development throughout the region. If we were going to defeat the Safeway development, we were going to have to defeat Owens and her efforts to promote unwanted development.

After one fruitless initial effort to negotiate with Owens, our group decided it was time for community "sprawl-buster training." Our approach was to turn out the community in mass, along with supportive elected officials and the media. The promotion for the event has become legendary among the environmental community. It was billed as "meet the monster that could eat South County." The promotional material and corresponding press releases promised a mystery guest, which was kept secret and only revealed to the press the afternoon prior to the event.

The *Washington Post, Baltimore Sun*, and *Capital* newspapers showed up to meet our mystery guest.[10] What they witnessed was a political ploy that would change the political fight against Safeway and leveled the playing field against developers for years to come. On the small bridge that crosses Rockhold Creek and overlooks Deale's historic fishing fleet, the mystery guest was revealed as a twelve-foot-high puppet, with a character likeness of our county executive, wearing a sash dubbing her "the Queen of Sprawl." The puppet was framed by a flock of protesters filling the bridge, creating a front-page photo opportunity for the local press.

From that moment forward the billion-dollar corporation that threatened our community and the county government that supported them were on the defensive. The media had a story it wanted to follow, and we used every opportunity to expose the inappropriateness of this project and its promoters. That evening a large crowd arrived at the meeting, literally filling the auditorium of the local elementary school. There, participants (including the president of the Maryland Senate, Mike Miller) received their sprawl-buster training. The biggest attraction of the event by far was the crowned papier-mâché effigy of Ms. Owens adorned with her now-famous sash labeling her "the Queen of Sprawl." The giant puppet was danced around the stage to the tune of Joni Mitchell's 1970s hit "Paradise." The group sang "you don't know what you've got till it's gone, they paved paradise and put up a parking lot." Now we were having fun; we were on the offensive and we were making progress.

The event empowered the community and was a media sensation. In turn, it heightened interest among several supportive elected officials. It also helped recruit new supporters to our cause and provided initial sprawl-buster training to our existing and new volunteers. From this point forward the campaign became quite intense, but we never lost sight of the "fun factor."

Our female supporters wore homemade earrings fashioned out of plastic Safeway shopping cards. Our handmade road signs gained attention by mixing humor and politics. One grocery cart–shaped sign read, "Miles of Aisles." Other signs, shaped like official road signs, read "For Sale: Our Future," "Entering Primary Growth Area: Resume Greed," and "Danger: Growth Zone Ahead." As quickly as the county took down our signs, we replaced them with new signs, and the media covered every move (*Baltimore Sun*, April 6, 1999).

Just in case the county officials had not heard our message, I took advantage of the often neglected public comment period that begins each of the county council's biweekly meetings. The rules of the council open the floor for two minutes to anyone in the community who would like to raise an issue of public concern. Rather than plead my case to the council, I used the time to deliver regular "Queen of Sprawl" reports. The sprawl reports were a chance to keep our issue front and center and to inform the council members of the county executive's latest efforts to install the sprawl. But county council chairwoman Shirley Murphy and the county executive's Office of Law saw things differently, and they worked hard to prevent me from delivering the reports.

Chairman Murphy was from the northern part of the county, and as a friend of Owens was doing everything she could to help the proposed Safeway project go forward. With the assistance of the ACLU's Baltimore office, I was allowed to continue delivering the reports, and to our benefit the media covered Murphy's unsuccessful effort to stifle my reports.[11] During her reelection campaign, we rented a passenger van and sent a team of seasoned volunteers to leaflet a Murphy fundraiser. It is impossible to say if the negative attention from our leafleting caused her reelection loss, but we certainly had fun informing her contributors how she was pushing sprawl into our community.

But our efforts did not stop there. With the new talent that SACReD had picked up along the way, including talented freelance writers, a one-page parody newsletter began to mysteriously appear at numerous locations throughout the region, including the waiting areas of the county's public offices. In blistering detail, the newsletter exposed the key county players and their plans, including a comedic explanation of the faux engineering model that the county was using to turn a floodplain into a non-floodplain so development could proceed in sensitive areas.

Another strategy of SACReD's multifaceted campaign was designed to enlarge and broaden the campaign against Safeway. Up to this point the Safeway issue had remained a local issue, with our side pushing our case and

Safeway firing back with a professional public relations campaign of their own that promised a modern new grocery store for our community. What they failed to show, however, was the impact of the eight additional store-fronts for national chain stores that would have evaporated our existing business community and displaced our town center. We needed to make the Deale Safeway proposal a wider public relations problem for the Safeway Corporation, so we engaged other Safeway stores in the region to harness their self-interest to benefit our cause.

At various Safeway store locations we distributed a leaflet entitled "Safeway Still Doesn't Get It" that made our case with a fact sheet, and ended with "Protect the Bay—No Deale Safeway." We started distributing the leaflet to shoppers in the general area, making sure that the store managers knew they had been leafleted, and then on a weekly basis moved out in larger distribution rings until we ended by leafleting stores in the District of Columbia. It was not long before store managers got our message and undoubtedly contacting the district office to find out why people were in front of their stores. This effort was brought to a head when we placed our community defenders in front of the nearby Edgewater Safeway with colorful homemade signs and handouts on a Saturday morning. So as not to use the store's parking lot, we bused our supporters to the store. The entire front sidewalk was filled with cheering, singing, and leafleting defenders of the Deale community, and there was nothing the corporation could do but take the heat.

While the public portion of the effort was moving forward with intensity, targeting the Safeway Corporation and Janet Owens and her supporters, others in our group were working closely with supportive state elected officials to craft protective legislation. For many environmental and engineering reasons, the storm water portion of the project was inappropriate for the headwaters of Rockhold Creek, but the developers' real problem was that they proposed draining their commercial storm water onto residential lots that Safeway had bought for this purpose. This concept had previously been deemed inappropriate by Maryland courts, and with Senate president Mike Miller on our side, legislation (Senate Bill 880) was quickly developed to deny such projects.

Now a race was on with the county. We could block the proposed development with new legislation, but in the meantime the county could approve the permitting and let the developer move forward with their project. Toward this end, the county issued a grading permit, which would allow bulldozers to begin grading despite the fact that the Environmental Protection Agency had asked the Army Corps of Engineers to suspend the existing wetlands permit. At this point, all the permits that the Safeway Corporation needed to begin bulldozing were in hand, and it seemed that it was only a matter of time before construction would begin on the strip mall.

Our frontline volunteers, many of whom had already been tested in tough demonstration situations, now showed up at the old Cedarhurst Community Center to receive formal training on nonviolent civil disobedience. The training was conducted by experts and lawyers in the area. For the next several weeks our activists "stood watch" for bulldozers. It looked as if we were going to have to physically block the bulldozers and possibly go to jail to buy the time we needed to pass the necessary legislation, a step many of us were willing to take—but the fun was over.

When the effort to stop the construction project appeared lost, the State Department of Natural Resources (DNR) stepped in and supported us by issuing a temporary halt to construction at the site. Miraculously, a nesting pair of bald eagles had been located near the site, and construction was delayed until after the end of the legal nesting season (June 15). You have to give credit to nature for defending its community, but Safeway's professional team suggested that SACReD was even behind the eagle nest. Their theory, shared with readers of the *Baltimore Sun*, stated, "[T]he head of the development company working for Safeway confided that some in Deale have suggested the nest might be a fake planted by foes to stop development."[12] While some would give us credit for the eagle nest, the truth is that nature had helped buy some time until we could pass a legislative fix that would keep commercial storm water devices and storm water off of residential property, and block this ill-conceived project.

In the end, it took passage of targeted state legislation on storm water and adoption of a new citizen-demanded down-zoning of the property in the county's Small Area Plan before all sides agreed that the project was dead. Our success could not have been achieved without the public awareness made possible through heightened media attention and the thousands of hours of volunteer community action. What we learned is that developers tend to go to the areas of least resistance and the defense of places like Deale, with its fishing and farming heritage, can be achieved if you are willing to fight like hell. Collaboration is nice, but if you want results, you better be willing to fight. What some developers learned is that there are easier places to bring their big box developments than the Shadyside Peninsula of Anne Arundel County.

But should unwelcome development arrive at our doorsteps again, rest assured that many of the citizens of our local community stand united to decide their own future. South Arundel Citizens for Responsible Development is proud to have built the first radio station in the nation owned and operated by an environmental organization (WRYR-LP 97.5 FM). The station has now been on the air for over five years and is 100 percent volunteer powered. The station empowers our community by celebrating the unique local character of our area and informing listeners of the latest issues. It also provides a forum for citizen dialogue and a platform to highlight the music of local performers.

Moreover, we are willing to keep the pressure on our elected officials. When Janet Owens attempted to restore her reputation following the Safeway debacle by undertaking a tour of the county to spread her folksy "I am looking out for you" message, we were there to offer a contrasting view.[13] Her public tour's southernmost stop was set for the Edgewater Senior Center, where our group met her with the Queen of Sprawl puppet. Though the county tour had been billed as a public event, when the county executive ventured toward the bottom of the county's sprawl line, close to our area, it became: ". . . submit questions in advance for an invitation only meeting," a fact that was covered by the local press.[14] As for the Queen of Sprawl puppet, SACReD sold it on eBay during Janet Owens's losing campaign for Maryland state comptroller, reminding the voters one more time of her "Install the Sprawl" record.

The Final Word

Guest entry by Bernie Fowler
Growing up on Broomes Island on the Patuxent River during the 1920s and '30s, my childhood and young adult life were a pleasant time for me. I have many good memories of that wonderful period, which I hold dear to this day. Crabs, oysters, fish, and clams were extremely abundant in those earlier years. The Patuxent River, the largest river totally in the state of Maryland and one of the major tributaries of our beautiful Chesapeake Bay, was the economic engine for most of us "Islanders."

Throughout the 1930s, we depended in large measure on this precious resource to supply most of the food and income needed to sustain us during the Great Depression. I vividly recall how productive and good the Patuxent River was to us at this critical time in history. While few of us had indoor plumbing or any other modern conveniences, when hunger and want were ever-present for many people in our country and people were lacking the bare necessities of life, we never went without. The Patuxent River, which I

often refer to as "The Beautiful Lady," was very generous to those of us who were fortunate enough to live along her shores.

After graduating from high school, I left the river for a tour of duty with the US Navy during World War II. Discharged in 1946, I returned to my beloved homeland and the shores of the Patuxent to start a boat rental business and work the water. At Bernie's Boat Rental on Broomes Island, I met and fell in love with a beautiful young lady who became my wife a year later. Betty and I will celebrate 60 years of happy marriage on September 9, 2009, and the Patuxent has been a part of our life together during every one of those years, which is another important reason I love the river.

I have a deep and abiding affection for the Patuxent and our Chesapeake Bay. I carry with me the memory of a once-productive river, a body of water that through the 1950s had water clarity as great as twelve feet deep. Sadly, few people today can even imagine, never mind remember, a healthy Patuxent. Today we measure the river's water clarity in inches, not feet, and the scientific community gave the Patuxent a grade of D- for water quality in 2009. It is important to remember that the Patuxent is not just a tributary of the Bay; it is a microcosm of the Bay. As the rivers go so shall the Bay.

Throughout my entire adult life, both within government in the Maryland State Senate (1983–1994) and on the Calvert County Commission (1970–1982) and outside of government, I have constantly and relentlessly fought to save this tributary of the Chesapeake Bay. Presently the news is discouraging, but that is not an acceptable excuse for our lack of effort. Drastic and immediate action is vital and absolutely necessary to avoid the death of one of the greatest estuaries in the world.

Please join me in refusing to forfeit your determination, hope, and optimism to restore the Bay. We know what is wrong. We know how to fix it. We ask our leaders to call on their conscience and listen to their hearts and show the courage and will to do what needs to be done now. It will not be easy but please, please waste no more time, a luxury we no longer have. And remember my motto, "Never give up, never, never, never give up!"

Notes

Preface

1. Emerson, Ralph Waldo. 1876. "Politics," reprinted (1987) in *Selected Essays*. New York: Penguin Books (pg. 422).

2. For a full list of fish consumption advisories in the six Bay states, see the Chesapeake Bay Program's website, www.chesapeakebay.net/fishadvisory.htm.

3. See the Chesapeake Bay Program's "Mycobacteriosis" for more on fish handler's disease. Available online, www.chesapeakebay.net/mycobacteriosis.aspx?menuitem = 19598.

4. See the Chesapeake Bay Program's "Is It Safe to Swim in the Bay?" Available online, www.chesapeakebay.net/bayfaq.aspx?menuitem = 14589#swim.

5. For beach advisories in Virginia, see the Virginia Department of Health (www .vdh.virginia.gov/Epidemiology/DEE/BeachMonitoring) and for beach advisories in Maryland waters, see Maryland Department of the Environment (www.mde.state.md .us/citizensinfocenter/health/beaches.asp).

6. See Virginia Department of Health, "Skin Infections Caused by Mycobacteria and Vibrio." Available online, www.vdh.state.va.us/epidemiology/DEE/Waterborne/skin infections.htm.

7. Fahrenthold, David. 2008. "The Crab Fishery Failure Declared." *Washington Post* (September 24, pg. B3).

Chapter 1: The Political Dead Zone

1. Leopold, Aldo. 1949 (reprinted 1970). *A Sand County Almanac (With Essays on Conservation from Round River)*. New York: First Ballantine Books Edition (pg. 263).

2. Clement, Chris, S. B. Bricker, and D. E. Pirhalla. 2001. "Eutrophic Conditions in Estuarine Waters." In *NOAA's State of the Coast Report*. Silver Spring, MD: National Oceanic and Atmospheric Administration. Available online, http://oceanservice.noaa.gov/ websites/retiredsites/sotc_pdf/EUT.PDF.

3. Diaz, Robert J. and Rutger Rosenberg. 2008. "Spreading Dead Zones and Consequences for Marine Ecosystems." *Science* (Vol. 321, No. 5891): pp. 926–29.

4. Lydersen, Kari. 2009. "Scientists Warn of Persistent 'Dead Zones' in Bay, Elsewhere." *Washington Post* (February 17, pg. A7).

5. Horton, Tom and William M. Eichbaum. 1991. *Turning the Tide: Saving the Chesapeake Bay*. Washington, DC: Island Press (pg. 18).

6. For a discussion of nutrient reduction techniques, see Ernst, Howard R. 2003. *Chesapeake Bay Blues: Science, Politics, and the Struggle to Save the Bay*. Lanham, MD: Rowman & Littlefield (pp. 53–88).

7. Layzer, Judith A. 2006. *The Environmental Case: Translating Values into Policy (Second Edition)*. Washington, DC: CQ Press (pp. 1–2).

8. See Boylan, Michael, ed. 2001. *Environmental Ethics: Basic Ethics in Action*. Upper Saddle River, NJ: Prentice Hall.

9. See Roundtree, Helen, Wayne Clark, and Kent Mountford. 2007. *John Smith's Chesapeake Voyages 1607–1609*. Charlottesville, VA: University of Virginia Press.

10. Steadman, David W. 2001. "A Long-Term History of Terrestrial Birds and Mammals in the Chesapeake-Susquehanna Watershed." In *Discovering the Chesapeake: The History of an Ecosystem*, ed. Philip D. Curtin, Grace S. Brush, and George W. Fisher. Baltimore: Johns Hopkins University Press (pg. 99).

11. Beatty, R. C. and W. J. Mulloy. 1940. *William Byrd's Natural History of Virginia or the Newly Discovered Eden*. Richmond, VA: Dietz Press.

12. Emerson, Ralph Waldo. 1987. *Selected Essays*. New York: Penguin Books.

13. Leopold, Aldo. 1949. *A Sand County Almanac* (reprinted 1990). New York: Ballantine Books (pp. 237–61).

14. For two excellent summaries of the deep ecology movement, see Paul Taylor's essay "Respect for Nature: A Theory of Environmental Ethics," pp. 49–53, and Arne Naess's essay "The Shallow and the Deep, Long-Range Ecology Movement: A Summary," pp. 248–59; both essays appear in Michael Boylan, ed. 2001. *Environmental Ethics: Basic Ethics in Action*. Upper Saddle River, NJ: Prentice Hall.

15. See Regan, Tom. 2000. *Defending Animal Rights*. Champaign, IL: University of Illinois Press.

16. Leopold, Aldo. 1949. *A Sand County Almanac* (reprinted 1990). New York: Ballantine Books. (pp. 237–62).

17. Foster, Catherine. 1991. "A Longtime Gadfly Still Stings." *Christian Science Monitor* (April 8 edition).

18. Earth Island Institute. *David Bower Legacy*. Available online, www.earthisland.org/index.php/aboutUs/legacy/ (accessed 02/26/09).

19. Horton, Tom (interview, February 7, 2009).

20. For an interesting discussion of this, see Kennedy, Robert F., Jr. 2005. *Crimes Against Nature*. New York: Harper Perennial (ch. 2).

21. See works like Brown, Edward R. 2008. *Our Father's World: Mobilizing the Church to Care for Creation*. Nottingham, England: InterVarsity Press; Berry, R. J., ed. 2000. *The Care of Creation: Focusing Concern and Action*. Nottingham, England: InterVarsity Press; Robinson, Tri and Jason Chatraw. 2006. *Saving God's Green Earth: Rediscovering the Church's Responsibility to Environmental Stewardship*. Boise, ID: Ampelon Publishing; and Sleeth, J. Matthew. 2007. *Serve God, Save the Planet: A Christian Call to Action*. Grand Rapids, MI: Zondervan.

22. See, Dryzek, John S. and David Schlosberg, eds. 1998. *Debating the Earth: The Environmental Politics Reader*. New York: Oxford University Press.

23. Malthus, Thomas Robert. 1798. *An Essay on the Principle of Population*. London: J. Johnson. Available online, www.econlib.org/LIBRARY/Malthus/malPop.html (accessed 03/18/09).

24. This idea is known as the environmental Kuznets curve, named after Simon Kuznets. Kuznets's theory concerns economic inequality and posits that inequality will increase as a country develops, but at some point it will level off and begin to decrease as the country continues to develop. Economists have used this work to suggest that developing countries, like China and India, are going though a rapid period of development that will have negative environmental consequence, but will ultimately reduce their environmental impact once they become more fully developed. For more on this, see Tisdell, Clement Allan. 2001. "Globalization and Sustainability: Environmental Kuznets Curve and the WTO. *Ecological Economics* 39 (pp. 185–96).

25. For a comprehensive view of CBF's institutional and political strategies, see Sherman, Jay (project director). 2000. *Building Blocks for Emerging Non-Profit Groups: Lessons from the Chesapeake Bay Foundation*. Annapolis, MD: Chesapeake Bay Foundation.

26. These calculations assume a 52-week year (with a 5-day and 40-hour workweek).

27. For quick facts about CBF, see www.cbf.org/site/PageServer?pagename = about _sub_mission_pr ofile (accessed 03/18/09).

28. For more on CBF's campaign for Captain John Smith, see Wood, Pam. 2008. "John Smith for President?" *The Capital* (June 21). Available online, www.hometownannapolis .com/news/env/2008/06/21-11/John-Smith-for-president.html (accessed 03/18/09).

29. For a list of the advocacy groups in the Bay watershed, see www.chesapeakebay.net/ findabaygroup.aspx?menuitem = 14797 (accessed 03/18/09).

30. Ernst, Howard R. 2003. *Chesapeake Bay Blues: Science, Politics, and the Struggle to Save the Bay*. Lanham, MD: Rowman & Littlefield (pg. 82).

31. Individual contributions can be searched through the Center for Responsive Politics' website (www.opensecrets.org) (accessed 03/18/09).

32. Section 117(g)(2)(A) of the Estuaries and Clean Water Act of 2000 states that only nonprofit groups are eligible for its grants.

33. For more information on these grants, see Chesapeake Bay Program: www.chesa peakebay.net/smallwatergrants.htm or National Fish and Wildlife Foundation: www .nfwf.org/AM/Template.cfm?Section = Chesapeake_Bay_Stewardship_Fund&Template = /TaggedPage/TaggedPageDisplay.cfm&TPLID = 46&ContentID;eq7547.

34. National Fish and Wildlife Foundation, www.nfwf.org/Content/NavigationMenu/ ChesapeakeBayStewardshipFund/ApplyforaGrant/default.htm.

35. Chesapeake Bay Commission. 2003. *The Cost of a Clean Bay*. Available online, www.chesbay.state.va.us/Publications/C2Kfunding.pdf.

36. For a description of the light green approach, see Environmental Protection Agency. 2005. *Community-Based Watershed Management Handbook*. EPA reference number EPA 842-B-05-003. Available online, www.epa.gov/neplessons/handbook.htm.

118 ᚛ Notes

37. Horton, Tom. 2003. *Turning the Tide: Saving the Bay (Revised and Expanded Edition).* Washington, DC: Island Press (pg. 5).

38. Horton, Tom. 2003. *Turning the Tide: Saving the Bay (Revised and Expanded Edition).* Washington, DC: Island Press (pg. 206).

39. Horton, Tom. 2003. *Turning the Tide: Saving the Bay (Revised and Expanded Edition).* Washington, DC: Island Press (pg. 208).

40. Fahrenthold, David A. 2007. "Wide-Open, Um, Plastic Spaces in Md." *Washington Post* (November 23, pg. A01).

41. While these claims are found in numerous Chesapeake Bay Program publications, for one example see "A 'Who's Who' In the Chesapeake Bay Program: 2003," pg. 1, available online from the Bay Program, www.chesapeakebay.net/pubs/whowho_2003.pdf (accessed 01/24/08).

42. Blankenship, Karl. 2008. "Bay Leaders Say They'll Not Meet 2010 Cleanup Goal." *Bay Journal* (Vol. 17, No. 10). Available online, www.bayjournal.com/article.cfm?article =3232 (accessed 01/24/08).

43. Government Accountability Office. "Improved Strategies Needed to Better Guide Restoration Efforts." GAO-06-614T. Available online, www.gao.gov/new.items/d06614t .pdf (accessed 01/24/08).

44. See EPA Office of Inspector General. 2008. *EPA Needs to Better Report Chesapeake Bay Challenges, A Summary Report* (Report No. 08-P-0199). Available online, www .epa.gov/oig/reports/2008/20080714-08-P-0199.pdf (accessed 09/05/08).

45. Chesapeake Bay Program. *2006 Annual Assessment.* Available online, www .chesapeakebay.net/indicators.htm (accessed 01/24/08).

46. See http://archive.chesapeakebay.net/index_cbp.cfm (accessed 09/05/08).

47. Source: Interview with Bay Program Director Jeffrey Lape (July 31, 2008, Eastport MD). See www.chesapeakebay.net/index_cbp.cfm (accessed 09/05/08).

48. See EPA Office of Inspector General. 2008. *EPA Needs to Better Report Chesapeake Bay Challenges, A Summary Report* (Report No. 08-P-0199). Available online, www.epa .gov/oig/reports/2008/20080714-08-P-0199.pdf (accessed 09/05/08).

49. The key findings of the symposium were published in eight separate essays that can be found in *Policy Studies Journal* 35 (November 2007): pp. 685–792 and *Policy Studies Journal* 36 (February 2008): pp. 61–166.

50. deLeon, Peter and Jorge E. Rivera. 2007. "Voluntary Environmental Programs: A Symposium." *Policy Studies Journal* 35 (November): pg. 685.

51. Koehler, Dinah A. 2007. "The Effectiveness of Voluntary Environmental Programs—A Policy at a Crossroads?" *Policy Studies Journal* 35 (November): pg. 689.

52. Lyon, Thomas P. and John W. Maxwell. 2007. "Environmental Public Voluntary Programs Reconsidered." *Policy Studies Journal* 35 (November): pg. 724.

53. Darnall, Nicole and Stephen Sides. 2008. "Assessing the Performance of Voluntary Environmental Programs: Does Certification Matter?" *Policy Studies Journal* 36 (February): pg. 110.

54. Rivera, Jorge E. and Peter deLeon. 2008. "Voluntary Environmental Programs: Are Carrots without Sticks Enough?" *Policy Studies Journal* 36 (February): pg. 63.

55. Rivera, Jorge E. and Peter deLeon. 2008. "Voluntary Environmental Programs: Are Carrots without Sticks Enough?" *Policy Studies Journal* 36 (February): pg. 61.

56. For more on the Tahoe Regional Planning Authority, see their website: www .trpa.org/default.aspx?tabindex = 0&tabid = 1 (accessed 02/03/08).

57. For the Tahoe Regional Planning Authority's data on the long-term water clarity trends of the lake, see www.trpa.org/default.aspx?tabindex = 0&tabid = 303 (accessed 02/03/08).

58. For more on this topic, see Muys, Jerome C., George William Sherk, and Marilyn C. O'Leary. 2007. "Utton Transboundary Resources Center Model Interstate Water Compact." *Natural Resources Journal* 47 (No. 1): pp. 18–115. Also see the Utton Transboundary Resource Center http://uttoncenter.unm.edu/model_compacts.html (accessed 01/27/09).

59. *New York v. New Jersey*, 256 U.S. 296, 313 (1921); *Texas v. New Mexico*, 462 U.S. 554, 575 (1983); and *Vermont v. New York*, 417 U.S. 270, 277 (1974).

60. See *The Delaware River Basin Commission Overview*. Available online, www.state .nj.us/drbc/over.htm.

61. Delaware River Basin Commission. 2008. *State of the Basin Report*. Available online, www.state.nj.us/drbc/SOTB/index.htm.

62. For an excellent example of federal government's push for environmental conflict resolution, see US Institution for Environmental Conflict Resolution. Information available online, http://ecr.gov (accessed 02/26/08).

63. For more on the collaborative voluntary approach being pursued for the Great Lakes, see Environmental Protection Agency, "A Strategy to Restore and Protect the Great Lakes." Available online, www.epa.gov/greatlakes/collaboration (accessed 3/4/08) and www.glrc.us/ (accessed 03/04/08).

64. For more on the collaborative voluntary approach being pursued for the Gulf of Mexico, see Environmental Protection Agency, "Mississippi River Basin and Gulf of Mexico Hypoxia." Available online, www.epa.gov/msbasin/index.htm (accessed 03/04/08).

65. As the Chesapeake Bay Program predates the National Estuary Program, it is not a participant in the program. However, the principles of the National Estuary Program are the same as those implemented by the Bay Program. For more on the National Estuary Program, see www.epa.gov/owow/estuaries/.

66. US Department of Energy. 2006. "Strategic Plan: U.S. Climate Change Technology Program." Washington DC: U.S. Department of Energy. Available online, www .climatetechnology.gov/stratplan/final/index.htm.

Chapter 2: Mismanaging the Commons

1. Emerson, Ralph Waldo. 1876. "Politics." Reprinted (1987) in *Selected Essays*. New York: Penguin Books (pg. 432).

2. See the Chesapeake Bay Program's description of the Atlantic menhaden in its

Bay Field Guide. Available online, www.chesapeakebay.net/bfg_atlantic_menhaden
.aspx(accessed 03/18/08).

3. Franklin, H. Bruce. 2001. "The Most Important Fish in the Sea: You've Never Heard of Them but Your Life May Depend on Them." *Discover: Science Technology and the Future* (September 1). Available online, http://discovermagazine.com/2001/sep/feat fish (accessed 03/18/08).

4. The 376-million-pound figure includes menhaden caught in the two states' coastal waters and the Bay. See Chesapeake Bay Program. 2008. *Atlantic Menhaden Harvest.* Available online, www.chesapeakebay.net/atlanticmenhadenharvest.aspx?menuitem = 14702 (accessed 09/17/08).

5. Blankenship, Karl. 2008. "Scientists Set Target of 200 Million Adults for Blue Crab Population." *Bay Journal* (Vol. 18, No. 1). Available online, www.bayjournal.com/ article.cfm?article = 3283.

6. Garrison and Link. 2002. Presentation to ASMFC Menhaden Technical Committee (10 July); Griffin, J. C. 2001. *Dietary Habits of an Historical Striped Bass Population in the Chesapeake Bay.* MS Thesis, University of Maryland Eastern Shore.

7. Jacobs, John M., et al. 2004. "Nutritional Health of Chesapeake Bay Striped Bass *Morone Saxatilis* in Relation to Disease." Presented at the 60th Annual Northeast Fish and Wildlife Conference. Ocean City, MD (April 27).

8. See Chesapeake Bay Program's description of mycobacteriosis. Available online, www.chesapeakebay.net/mycobacteriosis.aspx?menuitem = 19598 (accessed 03/18/08).

9. For more on human health concerns related to mycobacteriosis, see Maryland Department of Natural Resources recommendations. Available online, www.dnr.state .md.us/dnrnews/infocus/striped_bass_health.asp (accessed 03/18/08).

10. Blankenship, Karl. 2004. "Mycobacteriosis Infection Rate in Bay's Striped Bass Increasing." *Bay Journal* (Vol. 14, No. 4). Available online, www.bayjournal.com/article .cfm?article = 1252.

11. Asafu-Adjaye, John. 2005. *Environmental Economics for Non-Economists: Techniques and Policies for Sustainable Development (Second Edition).* Singapore: World Scientific Publishing (pg. 40).

12. This often-quoted phrase is from book IV, chapter 2 of Adam Smith's seminal work, *The Wealth of Nations* (1776). Full text available online, www.bibliomania.com/2/1/ 65/112/frameset.html (accessed 03/25/08).

13. Hanley, Nick, Jason F. Shogren, and Ben White. 1997. *Environmental Economics in Theory and Practice.* New York: Oxford University Press (pg. 22).

14. For more on market failures related to environmental economics, see Asafu-Adjaye, John. 2005. *Environmental Economics for Non-Economists: Techniques and Policies for Sustainable Development (Second Edition).* Singapore: World Scientific Publishing (pp. 63–103); and Hanley, Nick, Jason F. Shogren, and Ben White. 1997. *Environmental Economics in Theory and Practice.* New York: Oxford University Press (pp. 22–56).

15. For more on the problem of externalities, see Asafu-Adjaye, John. 2005. *Environmental Economics for Non-Economists: Techniques and Policies for Sustainable Development*

(Second Edition). Singapore: World Scientific Publishing (pp. 70–74); and Hanley, Nick, Jason F. Shogren, and Ben White. 1997. *Environmental Economics in Theory and Practice.* New York: Oxford University Press (pp. 29–37).

16. Hardin, Garrett. 1968. "The Tragedy of the Commons." *Science* 162: pp. 1243–48.

17. Dasgupta, Susmita, Benoit Laplante, Hua Wang, and David Wheeler. 2002. "Confronting the Environmental Kuznets Curve." *Journal of Economic Perspectives* 15, no. 1: pp. 147–68.

18. Clemons, Josh. 2003. "Supreme Court Rules for Virginia in Potomac Conflict." Published by the National Sea Grant Law Center. Available online, www.olemiss.edu/orgs/SGLC/National/SandBar/2.4supreme.htm.

19. Clifford, John. "Digging a Ditch toward a New Form of Government." Available online by the National Park Service, www.nps.gov/archive/thst/mtver.htm (accessed 01/24/08).

20. Wennersten, John R. 1981. *The Oyster Wars of Chesapeake Bay.* Centerville, MD: Tidewater Publishers.

21. Mountford, Kent. 2003. "No Matter What Shells Are Fired in Oyster Wars, The Resource Always Loses." *Bay Journal* (March). Available online, www.bayjournal.com/article.cfm?article=835 (accessed 01/24/08).

22. Ernst, Howard R. 2003. *Chesapeake Bay Blues: Science, Politics, and the Struggle to Save the Bay.* Lanham, MD: Rowman & Littlefield (pp. 107–108).

23. Virginia and Maryland have attempted two bistate working groups to manage the blue crab (one in the 1980s and one in the late 1990s). In both cases, the groups were disbanded after their proposals proved controversial in the respective states.

24. Ernst, Howard. 2003. "In Latest Struggle over Sensible Regulations, Crabs End Up Losers." *Bay Journal* (October). Available online, www.bayjournal.com/article.cfm?article=907.

25. The 2006 and 2007 harvests of blue crabs were two of the lowest on record. Chesapeake Bay Stock Assessment Committee. 2007. *2007 Chesapeake Bay Blue Crab Advisory Report.* Published by the National Oceanic and Atmospheric Administration and available online, http://chesapeakebay.noaa.gov/docs/2007bluecrabadvisoryreport.pdf (accessed 03/12/08). Blankenship, Karl. 2008. "Scientists Set Target of 200 Million Adults for Blue Crab Population." *Bay Journal* (March). Available online, www.bayjournal.com/article.cfm?article=3283 (accessed 03/12/08).

26. Chesapeake Bay Authority. 1933. *Chesapeake Bay Authority.* Conference proceedings from the Chesapeake Bay Authority meeting, October 6, Baltimore, MD (pp. 165–68).

27. US Corps of Engineers. 1973. *Chesapeake Bay Existing Conditions Report.* Baltimore: Army Corps of Engineers (Baltimore District).

28. US Corps of Engineers. 1977. *Chesapeake Bay Future Conditions Report.* Baltimore: Army Corps of Engineers (Baltimore District).

29. For an excellent documentary about Bernie Fowler's effort to save the Patuxent River, see Frank Cervarich's film, *Preacher for the Patuxent.* Capital City Communications. Potomac, MD.

30. For more on the Chesapeake Bay Commission, see www.chesbay.state.va.us/index .htm (accessed 01/24/08).

31. Fahrenthold, David A. 2008. "Optimism over Saving the Bay Bonded Local Jurisdictions." *Washington Post* (December 26).

32. Fahrenthold, David A. 2008. "Optimism over Saving the Bay Bonded Local Jurisdictions." *Washington Post* (December 26).

33. For more on the Chesapeake Bay Executive Council, see www.chesapeakebay.net/ exec.htm (accessed 01/24/08).

34. Following the initial Bay Agreement in 1983, the executive council has signed two additional Bay Agreements. The First Bay Agreement, little more than a paragraph in length, was a broad statement of intent to address the Bay's mounting problems. The 1987 agreement established 31 commitments (goals), and the 2000 agreement established 105 commitments (goals).

35. Article 1, Section 10 of the US Constitution prohibits any state "without the consent of Congress . . . [from entering] into any agreement or compact with another state." The Bay Agreements are not sanctioned by Congress, or even the various state legislatures; hence they do not violate the Constitution, but they also have no legal authority.

36. In 2009 the Chesapeake Bay Foundation, the region's leading environmental advocacy group, brought suit against the EPA, claiming that the Bay Agreements are in fact legally binding. The foundation based its argument in part on the fact that the Bay Program does receive federal money that is approved by Congress, making it a formal interstate compact. To date, no legal decision has been issued on this matter.

37. 1983 Chesapeake Bay Agreement. Available online, http://archive.chesapeake bay.net/pubs/1983ChesapeakeBayAgreement. pdf (accessed 03/13/08).

38. Chesapeake Bay Program staff list. Available online, www.chesapeakebay.net/ officestaff_alpha.aspx?menuitem = 14915 (accessed 03/13/08).

39. Chesapeake Bay Program committee structure. Available online, www.chesapeake bay.net/committeeactivities.aspx?menuitem = 14890 (accessed 03/13/08).

40. Alliance for the Chesapeake Bay. 2008. "Budget Highlights." *Bay Journal* (March). Available online, www.bayjournal.com/ (accessed 03/13/08).

41. See Chesapeake Bay Trust website for more information: www.cbtrust.org/ (accessed 03/13/08).

42. See the Alliance for the Chesapeake Bay website for more information: www.alliancechesbay.org/ (accessed 03/13/08).

43. See the Chesapeake Bay Foundation website for more information: www.cbf.org/ site/PageServer?pagename = homev3 (accessed 03/13/08).

44. See the Chesapeake Bay Program Organizational Structure. Available online, www.chesapeakebay.net/committeeactivities.aspx?menuitem = 14890 (accessed 03/13/ 08).

45. This claim was trumpeted by politicians throughout the watershed and repeated by news organizations. For one example of the claim, see Blankenship, Karl. 2000. "Executive Council Signs 'Historic' New Bay Pact." *Bay Journal* (July/August). Available online, www.bayjournal.com/article.cfm?article = 1300.

46. Ernst, Howard R. 2003. *Chesapeake Bay Blues: Science, Politics, and the Struggle to Save the Bay*. Lanham, MD: Rowman & Littlefield (pp. 63–64).

47. Blankenship, Karl. 1999. "Bay Program Mapping Road to Cleaner Bay." *Bay Journal* (November 1999). Available online, www.bayjournal.com/article.cfm?article = 1811.

48. For a good technical account of the Bay Program's various models, see Linker, Lewis C., Gary W. Shenk, Ping Wang, Katherine J. Hopkins, and Sjan Pokharel. 2001. "A Short History of Chesapeake Bay Modeling and the Next Generation of Watershed and Estuarine Models." Watershed 2002 Conference. Available online, www.ce.udel.edu/courses/CIEG667rader/Papers/Linker%20History%20of%20Ches%20Bay%20Modeling.pdf.

49. Pilkey-Jarvis, Linda and Orrin Jarvis. 2008. "Useless Arithmetic: Ten Points to Ponder When Using Mathematical Models in Environmental Decision Making." *Public Administration Review* (Vol. 68, No. 3): pp. 470–79.

50. Hanmer, Rebecca. 2004. "Numbers Count When Examining Chesapeake Cleanup Goals." *Bay Journal* (Vol. 14, No. 1). Available online, www.bayjournal.com/article.cfm?article = 1248.

51. Ernst, Howard. 2004. "Bay Program Must Account for Its Overestimated Numbers." *Bay Journal* (Vol 14, No. 2). Available online, www.bayjournal.com/article.cfm?article = 1285.

52. Ernst, Howard. 2008. "Useless Math or Dangerous Math?" *Public Administration Review* (Vol. 68, No. 3): pp. 46–50. Available online, www.aspanet.org/scriptcontent/custom/staticcontent/t2pdownloads/E rnstCommentary.pdf.

53. Hanmer, Rebecca. 2004. "Numbers Count When Examining Chesapeake Cleanup Goals." *Bay Journal* (Vol. 14, No. 1). Available online, www.bayjournal.com/article.cfm?article = 1248.

54. Horton, Tom and William M. Eichbaum. 1991. *Turning the Tide: Saving the Chesapeake Bay*. Washington, DC: Island Press (pg. 54).

55. Ernst, Howard R. 2003. *Chesapeake Bay Blues: Science, Politics, and the Struggle to Save the Bay*. Lanham, MD: Rowman & Littlefield (pg. 66).

56. Whoriskey, Peter. 2004. "Bay Pollution Progress Overstated: Government Program's Computer Model Proved Too Optimistic." *Washington Post* (July 18, pg. A01).

57. US Government Accountability Office (GAO). 2006. *Chesapeake Bay Program: Improved Strategies Needed to Better Guide Restoration Efforts*. Washington, DC: Government Printing Office. GAO-06-614T. Available online, www.gao.gov/new.items/d06614t.pdf.

58. Fahrenthold, David A. 2008. "Cleanup Estimate for Bay Lacking: EPA Program's Computer Formulas Called Optimistic." *Washington Post* (December 24, pg. B01).

59. Fahrenthold, David A. 2008. "Broken Promises on the Bay: Chesapeake Progress Reports Paint 'Too Rosy a Picture' as Pollution Reduction Deadlines Passed Unmet." *Washington Post* (December 27, pg. A01).

60. Fahrenthold, David A. 2008. "Broken Promises on the Bay: Chesapeake Progress Reports Paint 'Too Rosy a Picture' as Pollution Reduction Deadlines Passed Unmet." *Washington Post* (December 27, pg. A01).

61. Fahrenthold, David A. 2008. "Broken Promises on the Bay: Chesapeake Progress Reports Paint 'Too Rosy a Picture' as Pollution Reduction Deadlines Passed Unmet." *Washington Post* (December 27, pg. A01).

62. Pilkey-Jarvis, Linda and Orrin Jarvis. 2008. "Useless Arithmetic: Ten Points to Ponder When Using Mathematical Models in Environmental Decision Making." *Public Administration Review* (Vol. 68, No. 3): pp. 470–79.

63. Ernst, Howard. 2008. "Useless Math or Dangerous Math?" *Public Administration Review* (Vol. 68, No. 3): pp. 46–50. Available online, www.aspanet.org/scriptcontent/custom/staticcontent/t2pdownloads/E rnstCommentary.pdf.

64. Fahrenthold, David A. 2008. "Broken Promises on the Bay: Chesapeake Progress Reports Paint 'Too Rosy a Picture' as Pollution Reduction Deadlines Passed Unmet." *Washington Post* (December 27, pg. A01).

65. Fahrenthold, David A. 2008. "Broken Promises on the Bay: Chesapeake Progress Reports Paint 'Too Rosy a Picture' as Pollution Reduction Deadlines Passed Unmet." *Washington Post* (December 27, pg. A01).

66. Martin, Sandra Olivetti. 2004. "Making the Grade." *The Bay Weekly* (Vol. 12, Issue 34). Available online, www.bayweekly.com/year04/issuexii34/leadxii34.html (accessed 03/27/08).

67. Maryland's State Senator Brian Frosh, Maryland Delegate James Hubbard, and Virginia Delegate Albert Pollard.

68. Ernst, Howard R. 2003. *Chesapeake Bay Blues: Science, Politics, and the Struggle to Save the Bay.* Lanham, MD: Rowman & Littlefield (pg. 78).

69. Huslin, Anita. 2003. "Ehrlich Eases Liability for Big Chicken Firms: Maryland Drops Policy on Manure Runoff in Bay." *Washington Post.* (June 14, pg. A01).

70. Staff reporter. 2008. "Maryland Weakens New Poultry Regulations." *Bay Journal* (Vol. 18, No. 5, July-August). Available online, www.bayjournal.com/article.cfm?article =3381.

71. Fahrenthold, David A. 2008. "Md. Runs Short of Pollution Inspectors." *Washington Post* (September 23, pg. B01).

72. Glasser, Jessica. 2006. "Flush Tax Seen as Development Spur." *Associated Press* (September 9). Available online, www.wusa9.com/news/news_article.aspx?storyid= 52015.

73. Fahrenthold, David A. 2007. "Wide-Open, Um, Plastic Spaces in Md." *Washington Post* (November 23, pg. A01).

74. Wood, Pam. 2008. "Ruling Paves Way for Dobbins Island Development: River Group Can't Fight Zoning Approval." *The Capital* (July 15). Available online, www .hometownannapolis.com/cgi-bin/readne/2008/07_15-19/TOP.

75. Blankenship, Karl. 2003. "Bay Program Identifies 10 Most Key Restoration Goals to Meet." *Bay Journal* (Vol. 13, No. 6). Available online, www.bayjournal.com/article.cfm ?article = 1066.

76. Blankenship, Karl. 2006. "EPA Report Indicates 2010 Cleanup Deadline Will Not Be Met." *Bay Journal* (Vol. 16, No. 2). Available online, www.bayjournal.com/article.cfm ?article = 2775.

77. Blankenship, Karl. 2007. "Congress Creates Water Trail Marking Smith's Bay Journey." *Bay Journal* (Vol. 16, No. 10). Available online, www.bayjournal.com/article.cfm?article=2971.

78. The group was led by Gerald Winegrad and included Walter Boynton, Thomas Simpson, Will Dennison, Russ Brinsfield, Howard Ernst, Thomas Fisher, Gerrit-Jan Knaap, John Frece, Robert Etgen, Ned Gerber, Daniel Colhoun, Tom Horton, Richard Pritzlaff, Frances Flanigan, Charlie Steck, Jon Mueller, Senator Joe Tydings, and Bernie Fowler.

79. Not all participants at the December 3 meeting attended the December 8 press event.

80. Wood. Pam. 2008. "A Call for Bay Cleanup Reform." *The Capital* (December 8, pg. 1).

81. Halsey III, Ashley. 2009. "Obama Orders EPA to Take the Lead in Bay Cleanup." *Washington Post* (May 13, pg. A1).

82. Harper, Scott. 2009. "Obama Gives New Chesapeake Bay Cleanup a Boost." *The Virginian-Pilot* (May 13).

83. Springston, Rex. 2009. "Chesapeake Bay Cleanup to Be Speeded Up." *Richmond Times Dispatch* (May 13).

84. Halsey III, Ashley. 2009. "Obama Orders EPA to Take the Lead in Bay Cleanup." *Washington Post* (May 13, pg. A16).

Chapter 3: Who Will Tell the People?

1. Emerson, Ralph Waldo. 1836. "Nature." Reprinted (1987) in *Selected Essays*. New York: Penguin Books (pg. 36).

2. White, Christopher. 1989. *Chesapeake Bay Field Guide: Nature of the Estuary.* Centreville, MD: Tidewater Publishers (pg. 3).

3. Wennersten, John R. 1981. *The Oyster Wars of Chesapeake Bay.* Centerville, MD: Tidewater Publishers.

4. Horton, Tom and William M. Eichbaum. 1991. *Turning the Tide: Saving the Chesapeake Bay.* Washington, DC: Island Press (pg. 108).

5. Ernst, Howard R. 2003. *Chesapeake Bay Blues: Science, Politics, and the Struggle to Save the Bay.* Lanham, MD: Rowman & Littlefield (pg. 10).

6. Kennedy, Victor S. and Linda L. Breisch. 2001. *Maryland's Oysters: Research and Management.* University of Maryland (College Park), MD: A Maryland Sea Grant Publication (pg. xiii).

7. The two most common diseases now affecting the bay's oysters are Dermo and MSX.

8. Kennedy, Victor S. and Linda L. Breisch. 2001. *Maryland's Oysters: Research and Management.* University of Maryland (College Park), MD: A Maryland Sea Grant Publication.

9. Wieland, Robert. 2006. *Operating Costs in the Chesapeake Bay Oyster Fishery.*

Annapolis, MD: NOAA, Chesapeake Bay Office. Available online, www.mainstreet economics.com/documents/HarvestCostReport.pdf (accessed 01/29/09).

10. Newell, Roger I. E., Jeffrey C. Cornwell, and Michael S. Owens. 2002. "Influence of Simulated Bivalve Biodeposition and Microphytobenthos on Sediment Nitrogen Dynamics: A Laboratory Study." *Limnology and Oceanography* (Vol. 47, No. 5): pp. 1367–79. Available online, http://aslo.org/lo/toc/vol_47/issue_5/1367.pdf (accessed 01/29/09).

11. For an excellent case study on Love Canal, see Layzer, Judith A. 2006. *The Environmental Case: Translating Values into Policy (Second Edition)*. Washington, DC: CQ Press (ch. 3).

12. Brown, Michael. 1981. *Laying Waste: The Poisoning of America by Toxic Chemicals*. New York: Washington Square Press.

13. McNeil, Donald. 1978. "Upstate Waste May Endanger Lives." *New York Times* (August 2, section A1).

14. Layzer, Judith A. 2006. *The Environmental Case: Translating Values into Policy (Second Edition)*. Washington, DC: CQ Press (pp. 63–73).

15. See Kysar, Douglas A. 2008. "Book Review: The Consultant's Republic." *Harvard Law Review* (Vol. 121, June): pp. 2041–47.

16. Horton, Tom and William M. Eichbaum. 1991. *Turning the Tide: Saving the Chesapeake Bay*. Washington, DC: Island Press (pg. 54); Ernst, Howard R. 2003. *Chesapeake Bay Blues: Science, Politics, and the Struggle to Save the Bay*. Lanham, MD: Rowman & Littlefield (pg. 66).

17. Whoriskey, Peter. 2004. "Bay Pollution Progress Overstated: Government Program's Computer Model Proved Too Optimistic." *Washington Post* (July 18, pg. A01); Fahrenthold, David A. 2008. "Broken Promises on the Bay: Chesapeake Progress Reports Paint 'Too Rosy a Picture' as Pollution Reduction Deadlines Passed Unmet." *Washington Post* (December 27, pg. A01).

18. For more on the health risks related to radon, see EPA's website, www.epa.gov/radon/healthrisks.html and the University of Iowa's College of Public Health Studies, available online, www.cheec.uiowa.edu/misc/radon.html.

19. For more on state policies related to radon control, see the Environmental Law Institute's analysis on the subject, "Radon Control in New Home Construction: Developments in State Policy." Available online, www.eli.org/Program_areas/Radon/index.

20. Project for Excellence in Journalism. 2005. *State of the News Media, 2005*. New York: Columbia University (pg. 1).

21. Simon, David. 2009. "Testimony of David Simon." US Senate Committee on Commerce, Science, and Transportation Subcommittee on Communications, Technology, and the Internet (Hearing on the Future of Journalism). May 6.

22. For excellent coverage of this topic, see Wyss, Robert. 2008. *Covering the Environment: How Journalists Work the Green Beat*. New York: Routledge (pp. 150–52).

23. Wyss, Robert. 2008. *Covering the Environment: How Journalists Work the Green Beat*. New York: Routledge (pp. 250–51).

24. Wyss, Robert. 2008. *Covering the Environment: How Journalists Work the Green Beat*. New York: Routledge (pg. 252).

25. Project for Excellence in Journalism. 2008. *State of the News Media, 2008*. New York: Columbia University. Available online, www.stateofthenewsmedia.org/2008/narrative_overview_intro.php?media=1.

26. Simon, David. 2009. "Testimony of David Simon." US Senate Committee on Commerce, Science, and Transportation Subcommittee on Communications, Technology, and the Internet (Hearing on the Future of Journalism). May 6.

27. Simon, David. 2009. "Testimony of David Simon." US Senate Committee on Commerce, Science, and Transportation Subcommittee on Communications, Technology, and the Internet (Hearing on the Future of Journalism). May 6.

28. Project for Excellence in Journalism. 2008. *State of the News Media, 2008*. New York: Columbia University. Available online, www.stateofthenewsmedia.org/2008/narrative_overview_economics.php?cat=4& media=1.

29. Project for Excellence in Journalism. 2008. *State of the News Media, 2008*. New York: Columbia University. Available online, www.stateofthenewsmedia.org/2008/narrative_overview_newsinves tment.php?cat=6&media=1.

30. The survey of journalists was conducted September 17–December 3, 2007, among 585 reporters, editors, and news executives by the Pew Research Center for the People and the Press. Complete findings are available online, www.stateofthenewsmedia.org/2008/Journalist%20report%202008.pdf?cat=2&media; eq3.

31. Also see the Project for Excellence in Journalism. 2008. *State of the News Media, 2008*. New York: Columbia University. Available online, www.stateofthenewsmedia.org/2008/narrative_overview_intro.php?media=1.

32. Pew Research Center for the People & the Press. *Survey 2008*. Available online, www.stateofthenewsmedia.org / 2008 / Journalist%20report%202008.pdf?cat=2&media;eq3.

33. Fisher, Marc. 2009. "Bloggers Can't Fill the Gap Left by Shrinking Press Corps." *Washington Post* (March 1, pg. C1).

34. Fisher, Marc. 2009. "Bloggers Can't Fill the Gap Left by Shrinking Press Corps." *Washington Post* (March 1, pg. C4).

35. Wyss, Robert. 2008. *Covering the Environment: How Journalists Work the Green Beat*. New York: Routledge (pp. 8–9).

36. Friedman, Sharon M. 2004. "And the Beat Goes On: The Third Decade of Environmental Journalism." In Senecah, Susan L. (ed.) *The Environmental Communication Yearbook (Vol. 1)*. Mahwah, NJ: Lawrence Erlbaum Associates, Publishers.

37. Friedman, Sharon M. 2004. "And the Beat Goes On: The Third Decade of Environmental Journalism." In Senecah, Susan L. (ed.) *The Environmental Communication Yearbook (Vol. 1)*. Mahwah, NJ: Lawrence Erlbaum Associates, Publishers (pg. 176).

38. Friedman, Sharon M. 2004. "And the Beat Goes On: The Third Decade of Environmental Journalism." In Senecah, Susan L. (ed.) *The Environmental Communication Yearbook (Vol. 1)*. Mahwah, NJ: Lawrence Erlbaum Associates, Publishers (pp. 177–8).

39. The letter is available online, www.wfpl.org/CMS/?p=3167.

40. Shrogren, Liz. 2009. "The Future of Science and Environmental Journalism" pre-

sentation at the Woodrow Wilson International Center for Scholars, February 12. Available online, www.wilsoncenter.org/events/docs/Shogren%20Edited%20Transcript.pdf.

41. Borenstein, Seth. 2009. "The Future of Science and Environmental Journalism" presentation at the Woodrow Wilson International Center for Scholars, February 12. Available online, www.wilsoncenter.org/events/docs/Borenstein%20Edited%20Transcript.pdf.

42. Blankenship, Karl (interview, December 5, 2008).

43. West, Bernadette, Peter M. Sandman, and Michael R. Greenberg. 1995. *The Reporter's Environmental Handbook*. New Brunswick, NJ: Rutgers University Press (pg. 5).

44. Examples are taken from Peter Dykstra's presentation "The Future of Science and Environmental Journalism" at the Woodrow Wilson International Center for Scholars February 12, 2009. Available online, www.wilsoncenter.org/events/docs/Dykstra%20Edited%20Transcript.pdf.

45. Miller, Norman. 2002. *Environmental Politics: Interest Groups, the Media, and the Making of Policy*. New York: Lewis Publishers (pg. 55).

46. The logic employed in this section borrows heavily from Richard Fenno's classic study of congressional behavior. In his 1978 work (*Homestyles*), Fenno identifies the general goals of members of Congress and explains the various ways members view their constituency. Fenno explains how these views might affect congressional behavior and what it means for representative democracy. For more about Fenno's study, see Fenno, Richard. 1978. *Homestyles: House Members in Their Districts*. Boston: Little Brown. A useful summary of Fenno's argument is available online at the Social Science Summary Database, http://wikisum.com/w/Fenno:_Homestyle (accessed 02/05/09).

47. Horton, Tom (interview, February 7, 2009).

48. While some might argue that environmental journalists are torn between the competing goals of "advocacy reporting" and straight unbiased news coverage, less and less is the goal of advocacy a major force in mainstream environmental reporting. Environmental reporters today generally maintain the same level of professional objectivity that one would expect from other beats. For an interesting discussion on this topic, see Wyss, Robert. 2008. *Covering the Environment: How Journalists Work the Green Beat*. New York: Routledge (ch. 15). For the counterargument in environmental reporting, see Frome, Michael. 1998. *Green Ink: An Introduction to Environmental Journalism*. Salt Lake City, UT: University of Utah Press (part 1).

49. Simon, David. 2009. "Testimony of David Simon." US Senate Committee on Commerce, Science, and Transportation Subcommittee on Communications, Technology, and the Internet (Hearing on the Future of Journalism). May 6.

50. Miller, Norman. 2002. *Environmental Politics: Interest Groups, the Media, and the Making of Policy*. New York: Lewis Publishers (pg. 54).

51. Survey conducted for the California Academy of Sciences by Harris Interactive. 2009. Results are available online, www.topix.com/com/hpol/2009/03/american-adults-flunk-basic-science.

52. For recent information on the public's concern re: the environment, see Wyss,

Robert. 2008. *Covering the Environment: How Journalists Work the Green Beat.* New York: Routledge (pg. 8).

53. Wyss, Robert. 2008. *Covering the Environment: How Journalists Work the Green Beat.* New York: Routledge (pp. 70–71).

54. Miller, Norman. 2002. *Environmental Politics: Interest Groups, the Media, and the Making of Policy.* New York: Lewis Publishers (pp. 56–58).

55. Fahrenthold, David (interview, February 2, 2008).

56. Horton, Tom (interview, February 7, 2009).

57. Miller, Norman. 2002. *Environmental Politics: Interest Groups, the Media, and the Making of Policy.* New York: Lewis Publishers (pg. 56).

Chapter 4: Fighting for the Bay

1. Emerson, Ralph Waldo. 1843. "The Transcendentalist." Reprinted (1950) in *The Selected Writings of Ralph Waldo Emerson.* New York: The Modern Library College Editions (pp. 97–98).

2. Over the course of the struggle hundreds of individuals have helped to keep our campaign going. Some of these dedicated people include Peg Babyak, Paulette Berberich, Mary Hyde Berg, Glen Besa, Frank Bishop, Ann Brummer, Dori Chappell, Virginia Cowles, Kitty Cox, Frances Crutchfield, John Dawson, Tom Ellis, Leslie Fellows, Inez Fridley, Joanne Fridley, Sandra Fridley, Susan Gresham, Susan Garrett, Ed Gran, Bill Grant, Stephen Greenwood, the Henley Family, Ann Jennings, Sarah Kadec, Larkin Litton, Betsy and Dennis Mountcastle, Warren Mountcastle, John Moncrief, Ann Moore, Curt Moyer, William Perritts, Don Phillips, Kelly Place, Pete Rebick, Bob Richardson, Eugene Rivara, Garrie Rouse, Tom Rubino, Sharon Saari, Dawn Shank, Mike Siegel, Kay Slaughter, Ann Talley Shereen Waterlily, Ming and Ray Waters, and Karen Westermann.

3. Antonelli, Kris. 1999. "Tenacity Pays Off for Group." *Baltimore Sun* (August 1. pg. B1).

4. Albright, Scott. 1999. "Safeway to Meet with Opponents." *The Capital* (July 29).

5. Antonelli, Kris. 1999. "Legislators Back Demand for Hearing." *Baltimore Sun* (August 12, pg. B1).

6. Antonelli, Kris. 1999. "Legislators Back Demand for Hearing." *Baltimore Sun* (August 12, pg. B1).

7. Antonelli, Kris. 1999. "Group Wants Public Meeting." *Baltimore Sun* (October 1, pg. B1).

8. Mosk, Matthew. 2001. "There Is a Method to His Madness: Provocative Anti-Growth Activist Shay Gets Results." *Washington Post* (May 3, pg. T12).

9. Oakes, Amy. 1999. "Mall Foes Prepare Anew for Battle." *Baltimore Sun* (November 21, pg. B1).

10. Furgurson III, E. B. 2000. "Safeway Battle Rages, Opponents in Deale Mock Owens in Effigy." *The Capital* (October 10).

11. Calvert, Scott. 2001. "Council Aims to Boost Level of Decorum: Officials Consider Rules to Civility during Meetings." *Baltimore Sun* (February 7, pg. B1).

12. Calvert, Scott. 2000. "Eagle's Nest Delays Store Construction." *Baltimore Sun* (November 29, pg. B6).

13. Furgurson III, E. B. 2001. "Owens Hosts Local Forum." *The Capital* (March 1).

14. Furgurson III, E. B. 2001. "Owens Hosts Local Forum." *The Capital* (March 1).

References

Albright, Scott. 1999. "Safeway to Meet with Opponents." *The Capital* (July 29).

Ampelon Publishing and Sleeth, J. Matthew. 2007. *Serve God, Save the Planet: A Christian Call to Action*. Zondervan.

Antonelli, Kris. 1999. "Group Wants Public Meeting." *Baltimore Sun* (October 1, pg. B1).

Antonelli, Kris. 1999. "Legislators Back Demand for Hearing." *Baltimore Sun* (August 12, pg. B1).

Antonelli, Kris. 1999. "Tenacity Pays Off for Group." *Baltimore Sun* (August 1, pg. B1).

Asafu-Adjaye, John. 2005. *Environmental Economics for Non-Economists: Techniques and Policies for Sustainable Development (Second Edition)*. Singapore: World Scientific Publishing.

Beatty, R. C. and W. J. Mulloy. 1940. *William Byrd's Natural History of Virginia or the Newly Discovered Eden*. Richmond, VA: Dietz Press.

Berry, R. J., ed. 2000. *The Care of Creation: Focusing Concern and Action*. Nottingham, England: InterVarsity Press.

Blankenship, Karl (interview, December 5, 2008).

Blankenship, Karl. 2008. "Bay Leaders Say They'll Not Meet 2010 Cleanup Goal." *Bay Journal* (Vol. 17, No. 10). Available online, www.bayjournal.com/article.cfm?article = 3232.

Blankenship, Karl. 1999. "Bay Program Mapping Road to Cleaner Bay." *Bay Journal* (Vol. 9, No. 8). Available online, www.bayjournal.com/article.cfm?article = 1811.

Blankenship, Karl. 2000. "Executive Council Signs 'Historic' New Bay Pact." *Bay Journal* (Vol. 10, No. 5). Available online, www.bayjournal.com/article.cfm?article = 1300.

Blankenship, Karl. 2003. "Bay Program Identifies 10 Most Key Restoration Goals to Meet." *Bay Journal* (Vol. 13, No. 6). Available online, www.bayjournal.com/article.cfm?article = 1066.

Blankenship, Karl. 2004. "Mycobacteriosis Infection Rate in Bay's Striped Bass Increasing." *Bay Journal* (Vol. 14, No. 4). Available online, www.bayjournal.com/article.cfm?article = 1252.

Blankenship, Karl. 2006. "EPA Report Indicates 2010 Cleanup Deadline Will Not Be Met." *Bay Journal* (Vol. 16, No. 2). Available online, www.bayjournal.com/article.cfm? article = 2775.

Blankenship, Karl. 2007. "Congress Creates Water Trail Marking Smith's Bay Journey." *Bay Journal* (Vol. 16, No. 10). Available online, www.bayjournal.com/article.cfm?ar ticle = 2971.

Blankenship, Karl. 2008. "Scientists Set Target of 200 Million Adults for Blue Crab Population." *Bay Journal* (Vol. 18, No. 1). Available online, www.bayjournal.com/article .cfm?article = 3283.

Blankenship, Karl. 2009. "Court Rules Against Permit for Reservoir." *Bay Journal* (Vol. 19, No. 3).

Borenstein, Seth. 2009. "The Future of Science and Environmental Journalism" presentation at the Woodrow Wilson International Center for Scholars, February 12.

Boylan, Michael, ed. 2001. *Environmental Ethics: Basic Ethics in Action.* Upper Saddle River, NJ: Prentice Hall.

Brown, Edward R. 2008. *Our Father's World: Mobilizing the Church to Care for Creation.* Nottingham, England: InterVarsity Press.

Brown, Michael. 1981. *Laying Waste: The Poisoning of America by Toxic Chemicals.* New York: Washington Square Press.

Calvert, Scott. 2000. "Eagle's Nest Delays Store Construction." *Baltimore Sun.* (November 29, pg. B6).

Calvert, Scott. 2001. "Council Aims to Boost Level of Decorum: Officials Consider Rules to Civility During Meetings." *Baltimore Sun* (February 7, pg. B1).

Cervarich. Frank. 2008. "Preacher for the Patuxent." *Video Documentary.* Capital City Communications. Potomac, MD.

Chesapeake Bay Authority. 1933. *Chesapeake Bay Authority.* Conference proceedings from the Chesapeake Bay Authority meeting, October 6, Baltimore, MD (pp. 165–68).

Chesapeake Bay Commission. 2003. *The Cost of a Clean Bay.* Available online, www.ches bay.state.va.us/Publications/C2Kfunding.pdf.

Chesapeake Bay Program. 2006 *Annual Assessment.* Available online, www.chesapeake bay.net/indicators.htm.

Chesapeake Bay Program. 2008. *Atlantic Menhaden Harvest.* Available online, www.chesa peakebay.net/atlanticmenhadenharvest.aspx?menuitem = 14702.

Chesapeake Bay Program. 2009. *Committee Structure.* Available online, www.chesapeake bay.net/committeeactivities.aspx?menuitem = 14890.

Chesapeake Bay Program. 2009. *Staff List.* Available online, www.chesapeakebay.net/ officestaff_alpha.aspx?menuitem = 14915.

Chesapeake Bay Stock Assessment Committee. 2007. *2007 Chesapeake Bay Blue Crab Advisory Report.* Published by the National Oceanic and Atmospheric Administration and Available online, http://chesapeakebay.noaa.gov/docs/2007bluecrabadvisoryreport .pdf.

Clement, Chris, S. B. Bricker, and D. E. Pirhalla. 2001. "Eutrophic Conditions in Estuarine Waters." In *NOAA's State of the Coast Report*. Silver Spring, MD: National Oceanic and Atmospheric Administration. Available online, http://oceanservice.noaa.gov/websites/retiredsites/sotc_pdf/EUT.PDF.

Clemons, Josh. 2003. "Supreme Court Rules for Virginia in Potomac Conflict." Published by the National Sea Grant Law Center. Available online, www.olemiss.edu/orgs/SGLC/National/SandBar/2.4supreme.htm.

Clifford, John. "Digging a Ditch toward a New Form of Government." Available online by the National Park Service, www.nps.gov/archive/thst/mtver.htm.

Darnall, Nicole and Stephen Sides. 2008. "Assessing the Performance of Voluntary Environmental Programs: Does Certification Matter?" *Policy Studies Journal* 36 (February).

Dasgupta, Susmita, Benoit Laplante, Hua Wang, and David Wheeler. 2002. "Confronting the Environmental Kuznets Curve." *Journal of Economic Perspectives* 15, no. 1: pp. 147–68.

Delaware River Basin Commission. 2008. *State of the Basin Report*. Available online, www.state.nj.us/drbc/SOTB/index.htm.

deLeon, Peter and Jorge E. Rivera. 2007. "Voluntary Environmental Programs: A Symposium." *Policy Studies Journal* 35 (November).

Diaz, Robert J. and Rutger Rosenberg. 2008. "Spreading Dead Zones and Consequences for Marine Ecosystems." *Science* (Vol. 321, No. 5891): pp. 926–29.

Dryzek, John S. and David Schlosberg, eds. 1998. *Debating the Earth: The Environmental Politics Reader*. New York: Oxford University Press.

Dykstra, Peter. 2009. "The Future of Science and Environmental Journalism." Presentation at the Woodrow Wilson International Center for Scholars. February 12.

Earth Island Institute. *David Bower Legacy*. Available online, www.earthisland.org/index.php/aboutUs/legacy.

Emerson, Ralph Waldo. 1843. "The Transcendentalist." Reprinted (1950) in *The Selected Writings of Ralph Waldo Emerson*. New York: The Modern Library College Editions.

Emerson, Ralph Waldo. 1987. *Selected Essays*. New York: Penguin Books.

Environmental Protection Agency. 2005. *Community-Based Watershed Management Handbook*. EPA reference number EPA 842-B-05-003. Available online, www.epa.gov/neplessons/handbook.htm.

EPA Office of Inspector General. 2008. *EPA Needs to Better Report Chesapeake Bay Challenges, A Summary Report* (Report No. 08-P-0199). Available online, www.epa.gov/oig/reports/2008/20080714-08-P-0199.pdf.

Ernst, Howard R. 2003. *Chesapeake Bay Blues: Science, Politics, and the Struggle to Save the Bay*. Lanham, MD: Rowman & Littlefield.

Ernst, Howard. 2003. "In Latest Struggle Over Sensible Regulations, Crabs End Up Losers." *Bay Journal* (Vol. 13, No. 7). Available online, www.bayjournal.com/article.cfm?article=907.

Ernst, Howard. 2004. "Bay Program Must Account for Its Overestimated Numbers." *Bay Journal* (Vol. 14, No. 2). Available online: www.bayjournal.com/article.cfm?article=1285.

Ernst, Howard. 2008. "Useless Math or Dangerous Math?" *Public Administration Review* (Vol. 68, No. 3): pp. 46–50. Available online, www.aspanet.org/scriptcontent/custom/staticcontent/t2pdownloads/E rnstCommentary.pdf.

Fahrenthold, David A. 2007. "Wide-Open, Um, Plastic Spaces in Md." *Washington Post* (November 23, pg. A01).

Fahrenthold, David (interview, February 2, 2008).

Fahrenthold, David. 2008. "The Crab Fishery Failure Declared." *Washington Post* (September 24, pg. B3).

Fahrenthold, David A. 2008. "Broken Promises on the Bay: Chesapeake Progress Reports Paint 'Too Rosy a Picture' as Pollution Reduction Deadlines Passed Unmet." *Washington Post* (December 27, pg. A01).

Fahrenthold, David A. 2008. "Cleanup Estimate for Bay Lacking: EPA Program's Computer Formulas Called Optimistic." *Washington Post* (December 24, pg. B01).

Fahrenthold, David A. 2008. "Md. Runs Short of Pollution Inspectors." *Washington Post* (September 23, pg. B01).

Fahrenthold, David A. 2008. "Optimism Over Saving the Bay Bonded Local Jurisdictions." *Washington Post* (December 26).

Fenno, Richard. 1978. *Homestyles: House Members in Their Districts*. Boston: Little Brown.

Fisher, Marc. 2009. "Bloggers Can't Fill the Gap Left by Shrinking Press Corps." *Washington Post* (March 1, pg. C1).

Foster, Catherine. 1991. *Christian Science Monitor* (April 8 edition).

Franklin, H. Bruce. 2001. "The Most Important Fish in the Sea: You've Never Heard of Them but Your Life May Depend on Them." *Discover: Science Technology and the Future* (September 1). Available online, http://discovermagazine.com/2001/sep/featfish.

Friedman, Sharon M. 2004. "And the Beat Goes On: The Third Decade of Environmental Journalism." In Senecah, Susan L., ed. *The Environmental Communication Yearbook (Volume 1)*. Mahwah, NJ: Lawrence Erlbaum Associates, Publishers.

Frome, Michael. 1998. *Green Ink: An Introduction to Environmental Journalism*. Salt Lake City, UT: University of Utah Press.

Furgurson III, E. B. 2000. "Safeway Battle Rages, Opponents in Deale Mock Owens in Effigy." *The Capital* (October 10).

Furgurson III, E. B. 2001. "Owens Hosts Local Forum." *The Capital* (March 1).

Garrison and Link. 2002. Presentation to ASMFC Menhaden Technical Committee (July 10).

Glasser, Jessica. 2006. "Flush Tax Seen as Development Spur." *Associated Press* (September 9). Available online, www.wusa9.com/news/news_article.aspx?storyid = 52015.

Government Accountability Office. 2006. *Chesapeake Bay Program: Improved Strategies Needed to Better Guide Restoration Efforts*. GAO-06-614T. Available online, www.gao.gov/new.items/d06614t.pdf (accessed 01/24/08).

Griffin, J. C. 2001. *Dietary Habits of an Historical Striped Bass Population in the Chesapeake Bay*. MS Thesis, University of Maryland Eastern Shore.

Halsey III, Ashley. 2009. "Obama Orders EPA to Take the Lead in Bay Cleanup." *Washington Post* (May 13, pg. A1).

Hanley, Nick, Jason F. Shogren, and Ben White. 1997. *Environmental Economics in Theory and Practice*. New York: Oxford University Press.

Hanmer, Rebecca. 2004. "Numbers Count When Examining Chesapeake Cleanup Goals." *Bay Journal* (Vol. 14, No. 1). Available online, www.bayjournal.com/article.cfm?article=1248.

Hardin, Garrett. 1968. "The Tragedy of the Commons." *Science* (Vol. 162): pp. 1243–48.

Harper, Scott. 2009. "Obama Gives New Chesapeake Bay Cleanup a Boost." *The Virginian-Pilot* (May 13).

Horton, Tom (interview, February 7, 2009).

Horton, Tom and William M. Eichbaum. 1991. *Turning the Tide: Saving the Chesapeake Bay*. Washington, DC: Island Press.

Horton, Tom. 2003. *Turning the Tide: Saving the Bay (Revised and Expanded Edition)*. Washington, DC: Island Press.

Huslin, Anita. 2003. "Ehrlich Eases Liability for Big Chicken Firms: Maryland Drops Policy on Manure Runoff in Bay." *Washington Post* (June 14, pg. A01).

Interview with Bay Program Director Jeffrey Lape (July 31, 2008, Eastport, MD).

Jacobs, John M., et al. 2004. "Nutritional Health of Chesapeake Bay Striped Bass *Morone Saxatilis* in Relation to Disease." Presented at the 60th Annual Northeast Fish and Wildlife Conference. Ocean City, MD (April 27).

Kennedy, Robert F., Jr. 2005. *Crimes Against Nature*. New York: Harper Perennial.

Kennedy, Victor S. and Linda L. Breisch. 2001. *Maryland's Oysters: Research and Management*. University of Maryland (College Park), MD: A Maryland Sea Grant Publication.

Koehler, Dinah A. 2007. "The Effectiveness of Voluntary Environmental Programs—A Policy at a Crossroads?" *Policy Studies Journal* 35 (November).

Kysar, Douglas A. 2008. "Book Review: The Consultant's Republic." *Harvard Law Review* (Vol. 121, June): pp. 2041–47.

Layzer, Judith A. 2006. *The Environmental Case: Translating Values into Policy (Second Edition)*. Washington, DC: CQ Press.

Leopold, Aldo. 1949 (reprinted 1990). *A Sand County Almanac (With Essays on Conservation from Round River)*. New York: First Ballantine Books Edition.

Linker, Lewis C., Gary W. Shenk, Ping Wang, Katherine J. Hopkins, and Sjan Pokharel. 2001. "A Short History of Chesapeake Bay Modeling and the Next Generation of Watershed and Estuarine Models." Watershed 2002 Conference. Available online, www.ce.udel.edu/courses/CIEG667rader/Papers/Linker%20History%20of%20Ches%20Bay%20Modeling.pdf.

Lydersen, Kari. 2009. "Scientists Warn of Persistent 'Dead Zones' in Bay, Elsewhere." *Washington Post* (February 17, pg. A7).

Lyon, Thomas P. and John W. Maxwell. 2007. "Environmental Public Voluntary Programs Reconsidered." *Policy Studies Journal* 35 (November).

Malthus, Thomas Robert. 1798. *An Essay on the Principle of Population*. London: J. Johnson. Available online, www.econlib.org/LIBRARY/Malthus/malPop.html.

Martin, Sandra Olivetti. 2004. "Making the Grade." *The Bay Weekly* (Vol. 12, No. 34). Available online, www.bayweekly.com/year04/issuexii34/leadxii34.html.

McNeil, Donald. 1978. "Upstate Waste May Endanger Lives." *New York Times* (August 2, section A1).

Miller, Norman. 2002. *Environmental Politics: Interest Groups, the Media, and the Making of Policy.* New York: Lewis Publishers.

Mosk, Matthew. 2001. "There Is a Method to His Madness: Provocative Anti-Growth Activist Shay Gets Results." *Washington Post* (May 3, pg. T12).

Mountford, Kent. 2003. "No Matter What Shells Are Fired in Oyster Wars, the Resource Always Loses." *Bay Journal* (Vol. 13, No. 1). Available online, www.bayjournal.com/article.cfm?article = 835.

Muys, Jerome C., George William Sherk, and Marilyn C. O'Leary. 2007. "Utton Transboundary Resources Center Model Interstate Water Compact." *Natural Resources Journal* (Vol. 47, No. 1): pp. 18–115.

Naess, Arne. 2001. "The Shallow and the Deep, Long-Range Ecology Movement: A Summary," In Michael Boylan, ed. 2001. *Environmental Ethics: Basic Ethics in Action.* Upper Saddle River, NJ: Prentice Hall.

Newell, Roger I. E., Jeffrey C. Cornwell, and Michael S. Owens. 2002. "Influence of Simulated Bivalve Biodeposition and Microphytobenthos on Sediment Nitrogen Dynamics: A Laboratory Study." *Limnology and Oceanography* (Vol. 47, No. 5): pp. 1367–79. Available online, http://aslo.org/lo/toc/vol_47/issue_5/1367.pdf.

Oakes, Amy. 1999. "Mall Foes Prepare Anew for Battle." *Baltimore Sun* (November 21, pg. B1).

Pilkey-Jarvis, Linda and Orrin Jarvis. 2008. "Useless Arithmetic: Ten Points to Ponder When Using Mathematical Models in Environmental Decision Making." *Public Administration Review* (Vol 68, No. 3): pp. 470–79.

Project for Excellence in Journalism. 2005. *State of the News Media, 2005.* New York: Columbia University.

Project for Excellence in Journalism. 2008. *State of the News Media, 2008.* New York: Columbia University. Available online, www.stateofthenewsmedia.org/2008/narrative_overview_intro.php?media = 1.

Regan, Tom. 2000. *Defending Animal Rights.* Champaign, IL: University of Illinois Press.

Rivera, Jorge E. and Peter deLeon. 2008. "Voluntary Environmental Programs: Are Carrots without Sticks Enough?" *Policy Studies Journal* 36 (February).

Robinson, Tri and Jason Chatraw. 2006. *Saving God's Green Earth: Rediscovering the Church's Responsibility to Environmental Stewardship.* Grand Rapids, MI: Zondervan.

Roundtree, Helen, Wayne Clark, and Kent Mountford. 2007. *John Smith's Chesapeake Voyages 1607–1609.* Charlottesville, VA: University of Virginia Press.

Sherman, Jay (project director). 2000. *Building Blocks for Emerging Non-Profit Groups: Lessons from the Chesapeake Bay Foundation.* Annapolis, MD: Chesapeake Bay Foundation.

Shrogren, Liz. 2009. "The Future of Science and Environmental Journalism" presentation at the Woodrow Wilson International Center for Scholars, February 12.

Simon, David. 2009. "Testimony of David Simon." US Senate Committee on Commerce, Science, and Transportation Subcommittee on Communications, Technology, and the Internet (Hearing on the Future of Journalism). May 6.

Sleeth, J. Matthew. 2007. *Serve God, Save the Planet: A Christian Call to Action.* Grand Rapids, MI: Zondervan.

Springston, Rex. 2009. "Chesapeake Bay Cleanup to Be Speeded Up." *Richmond Times Dispatch* (May 13).

Staff reporter. 2008. "Maryland Weakens New Poultry Regulations" *Bay Journal* (Vol. 18, No. 5). Available online, www.bayjournal.com/article.cfm?article=3381.

Steadman, David W. 2001. "A Long-Term History of Terrestrial Birds and Mammals in the Chesapeake-Susquehanna Watershed." In *Discovering the Chesapeake: The History of an Ecosystem,* ed. Philip D. Curtin, Grace S. Brush, and George W. Fisher. Baltimore: Johns Hopkins University Press.

Taylor, Paul. 2001. "Respect for Nature: A Theory of Environmental Ethics," In Michael Boylan, ed. 2001. *Environmental Ethics: Basic Ethics in Action.* Upper Saddle River, NJ: Prentice Hall.

Tisdell, Clement Allan. 2001. "Globalization and Sustainability: Environmental Kuznets Curve and the WTO." *Ecological Economics* 39.

US Corps of Engineers. 1973. *Chesapeake Bay Existing Conditions Report.* Baltimore: Army Corps of Engineers (Baltimore District).

US Corps of Engineers. 1977. *Chesapeake Bay Future Conditions Report.* Baltimore: Army Corps of Engineers (Baltimore District).

Wennersten, John R. 1981. *The Oyster Wars of Chesapeake Bay.* Centerville, MD: Tidewater Publishers.

West, Bernadette, Peter M. Sandman, and Michael R. Greenberg. 1995. *The Reporter's Environmental Handbook.* New Brunswick, NJ: Rutgers University Press.

White, Christopher P. 1989. *Chesapeake Bay: A Field Guide.* Centreville, MD: Tidewater Publishers.

White, Christopher. 1989. *Chesapeake Bay Field Guide: Nature of the Estuary.* Centreville, MD: Tidewater Publishers (pg. 3).

Whoriskey, Peter. 2004. "Bay Pollution Progress Overstated: Government Program's Computer Model Proved Too Optimistic." *Washington Post* (July 18, pg. A01).

Wieland, Robert. 2006. *Operating Costs in the Chesapeake Bay Oyster Fishery.* Annapolis, MD: NOAA, Chesapeake Bay Office. Available online, www.mainstreeteconomics .com/documents/HarvestCostReport.pdf.

Wood, Pamela. 2008. "A Call for Bay Cleanup Reform." *The Capital* (December 8, pg. 1).

Wood, Pamela. 2008. "John Smith for President?" *The Capital* (June 21). Available online, www.hometownannapolis.com/news/env/2008/06/21-11/John-Smith-for-president.html.

Wood, Pamela. 2008. "Ruling Paves Way for Dobbins Island Development: River Group Can't Fight Zoning Approval." *The Capital* (July 15).

Wyss, Robert. 2008. *Covering the Environment: How Journalists Work the Green Beat.* New York: Routledge.

Index

About the Author

Howard Ernst lives in Annapolis, Maryland, where he is an associate profes-sor of political science at the United States Naval Academy and a senior scholar at the University of Virginia's Center for Politics. The views expressed in this book are his alone. Professor Ernst welcomes your com-ments and suggestions (*www.howardernst.com*).

WITHDRAWN

39.95   1/13/10